ARCHITECTURAL
DRAWINGS OF THE
REGENCY PERIOD

1790–1837

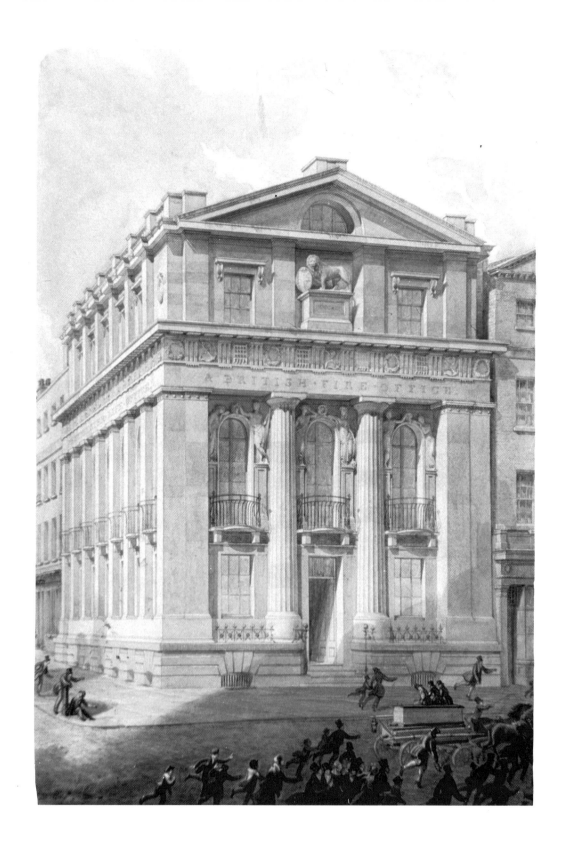

Frontispiece: **Charles Robert Cockerell 1788–1863**
Design for the Westminster Life and British Fire Office, Strand, Westminster
Perspective, 1831. Pen, pencil and watercolour (540 × 395)

ARCHITECTURAL DRAWINGS OF THE REGENCY PERIOD

1790–1837

Giles Worsley

From the Drawings Collection of the
Royal Institute of British Architects

SERIES EDITOR, JILL LEVER

ANDRE DEUTSCH

For B W

First published in 1991 by
André Deutsch Limited
105-106 Great Russell Street
London WC1B 3LJ

British Library Cataloguing in Publication Data
Royal Institute of British Architects, Drawings Collection
Architectural drawings of the Regency period: from the Drawings
Collection British Architectural Library, Royal Institute of British
Architects.
1. British Architectural drawings, 1500–1981 – Illustrations
I. Title   II. Worsley, Giles
720.22241

ISBN 0–233–98625–1
ISBN 0–233–98626 X pbk

Phototypeset by Falcon Graphic Art Ltd
Wallington, Surrey
Printed and bound in Singapore by
Kim Hup Lee

ACKNOWLEDGEMENTS

My chief thanks must lie with Jill Lever, Curator of the RIBA Drawings Collection for asking me to write this book, and to all the staff of the Collection, particularly Dr Neil Bingham, Tim Knox and Andrew Norris for their help and forbearance. Jill Lever kindly read the text, as did Margaret Richardson and my colleague Michael Hall, and their comments, together with those of John Newman, are gratefully acknowledged. I must also thank the staff of the RIBA Library whose Manuscripts Collection has been invaluable.

CONTENTS

PREFACE

REGENCY architecture has never been very fashionable, although Regency decoration and furniture have had their moments. It forms a no-man's-land between two popular schools of architectural appreciation, between those who love the ordered beauty of the eighteenth century and those who seek the muscular certainties of the nineteenth century. A vague air of disrepute, of stylistic insincerity and shoddy construction hang over the whole period. To scholars bred in the age of modernist certainty there had to be something wrong about architects like James Wyatt or his nephew Sir Jeffry Wyatville who were happy to design in any style. Nash's relaxed attitude to the orders seems to cast a pall over an entire age. The reputation of the Commissioners' churches has never recovered from the savaging of Pugin's ideological crusade. But to damn the architecture of an age because it fails to fit in with the prejudices of later generations is to deny it justice.

That Wyatt and his successors could design in any number of styles does not mean those styles are meretricious. That the Gothic of the Commissioners' churches, of Rickman or Vulliamy, is not an exact copy of that of medieval churches does not mean that it is invalid. In fact Regency architecture has great buildings as intellectually rigorous as those of any age: Thomas Harrison at Chester Castle, Charles Cockerell at the Westminster Life and British Fire Office, Sir John Soane at the Bank of England. Nor is it fair to condemn the Regency as a time of shoddy construction. Every age has had its fair share of bad building, but the architecture of Sir Robert Smirke was distinguished by the excellence of its construction, while the stonework at Sir Jeffry Wyatville's Chatsworth would be hard to beat at any date.

Of course, all this begs the question of what we mean by Regency architecture. Descriptive labels seldom sit entirely happily on any period of architecture, and this remains true of 'Regency'. Technically, the Regency ran from 1811 to 1820, but the word has come to be accepted as covering a rough period from approximately 1790 to 1837. The nine years between 1788 and 1796 saw the deaths of four of the five architects who had dominated British architecture since the 1750s, Sir Robert Taylor, James Paine, Robert Adam and Sir William Chambers. Only James Wyatt worked on, and his omniverous ability always seems more in sympathy with the Regency. With their deaths died the Palladian orthodoxy that had prevailed, through many twists and turns, for nearly three-quarters of a century. In its place came the Greek Revival heralded by Thomas Harrison's Chester Castle begun in 1788. Even more significant were the publications in 1794 of Richard Payne Knight's *The Landscape, A Didactic Poem,* and Uvedale Price's *An Essay on the Picturesque,* for the picturesque, with its concentration on visual qualities in architecture, dominates the Regency.

The year 1837 saw the accession of the new queen, but more significantly for architecture the presentation of a royal charter to the new Institute of British Architects, the final seal on the struggle for professional status that had preoccupied architects during the Regency. This ushered in the solid respectability of the Victorian architectural profession, in the year that Soane, who had fought so long for that respectability, died. The same year saw the death of James Burton, the builder who had made so much of Regency London possible, two years after the death of John Nash, who owed so much to him. Nash was the archetype of the sort of Regency architect that Soane distrusted, part architect, part speculator, part builder. The late 1830s did not see a complete cull of the Regency profession, in fact it is remarkable how many of the key figures, Cockerell, Dobson, Smirke, Barry, Fowler, J.A. Repton, lived on into the 1860s. Decimus Burton, who had designed the Athenaeum in 1827, did not die until 1881. But the death of Regency architecture can really be dated to 1836 and the publication of A.W.N. Pugin's *Contrasts: or, A Parallel Between the Noble Edifices of the Fourteenth and Fifteenth Centuries, and similar Buildings of the Present Day; Showing the Present Decay of Taste: Accompanied by appropriate Text*. It would no longer be possible to design solely with an eye to the picturesque.

But if the significance of Regency architecture remains debatable, there can be no denying the fact that it was one of the great ages of architectural draughtsmanship: an age of rapid change and one of great beauty. The perspectives of Joseph Bonomi and J.M. Gandy would have held their own against most of the paintings and watercolours among which they were hung at the Royal Academy. It was an age in which draughtsmanship was taken very seriously, with different drawings playing different roles: design drawings, presentation drawings, working drawings, record drawings. To understand the role architectural drawings played it is important to distinguish these different sorts of drawings.

All the drawings illustrated in this book come from the Drawings Collection of the Royal Institute of British Architects, but despite the breadth of the Collection there are inevitable gaps. A complete account of the period would have to have included the drawings of the Soane Museum, for there are only a handful of drawings by Soane and virtually none by George Dance. More worrying is the partial view of architecture the collection presents. These years were years of war and commercial expansion and yet no drawings survive of barrack building, and the great dock developments of London and Liverpool are unrepresented.

Within these constraints the drawings chosen try to give a representative account of contemporary architecture, from the grandest public building to the most humble terraced house; from the work of the most famous architects to that of the least known; from the most beautiful perspectives to the simplest survey plan. The result is not a comprehensive account of Regency architecture, but an insight into the architecture of that age through its drawings. To set this in its perspective the introduction attempts to sketch the character of the architectural profession in the Regency, relying primarily on contemporary papers and biographies. More needs to be done. Margaret Richardson's anticipated account of Soane's office will shed much light, but the key to this book lies in its colour. For too long it has been accepted that architectural drawings are published in black and white. The result has been a serious distortion for it is impossible to understand the role of architectural drawings, during the Regency at least, if they are not shown in colour.

INTRODUCTION
ARCHITECTURE AND THE ARCHITECTURAL PROFESSION DURING THE REGENCY

War and then peace divide the Regency period neatly down the middle, nearly quarter of a century of war followed by quarter of a century of a peace that would stretch virtually unbroken for almost a hundred years. From 1793 to 1815 England was in a permanent state of war with France, except for brief respites during the Peace of Amiens in 1802-03, and after Napoleon's initial abdication in 1814. Money was tight, taxes high. Civic architecture was minimal, speculative urban building slow, country house building severely affected. But the demands of long-term global war were reflected in the rebuilding of the Royal Mint and the Bank of England, and in the vast sums spent on barracks and naval installations. At the same time booming trade with the rest of the world led to the erection of the first great commercial docks in London, and the need for armaments boosted rapid industrialisation.

Peace saw a quarter of a century's pent-up demand let loose. Enormous profits made out of the war were poured into speculative housing and villas for the newly rich. Agriculture flourished, and with it country house building. Public spending, reserved so long for the demands of war, turned with a vengeance to civic architecture, monuments, bridges over the Thames, a royal palace, museums, hospitals, schools, a myriad of churches under the Million Pound Act, all served to change the face of London and the major cities in a manner that foreigners found astounding.

But peace brought a return to the cycle of boom and crash that had been masked by war. The great stop of 1825 saw innumerable banks fail and large numbers of speculative builders bankrupted. Nothing, however, could stop the confident onward march of the British economy, fuelled by the industrial revolution, and with it the British architectural profession. These were good years for architects. While there might be periods of shortage, the demand for architects was expanding as never before. Substantial fortunes were there to be made, not from contracting as earlier, but from designing and supervising the erection of buildings. By 1837 the concept of an architect as a professional supervisor, separate from the builder, had been established, a concept sealed in the royal charter given that year to the Institute of British Architects which had been founded in 1834. This was later to become the Royal Institute of British Architects.

For the architectural profession the Regency was a period of consolidation not of innovation. The years of innovation had been the decades after 1750 when architects like Sir William Chambers, the Adam brothers, Sir Robert Taylor, James Paine, Henry Holland and George Dance had established large well-run offices with properly trained pupils and had introduced new techniques of draughtsmanship. It was the practices established in these offices that gradually became standard for Regency architects. In the absence of a comprehensive account of them it will be necessary to touch briefly on some of these developments, but a fuller account will have to wait for a subsequent volume in this series.

Henry Flitcroft, one of the most successful mid-eighteenth century architects, made do with a single assistant. At least ten worked at different times under Chambers, eight under Taylor and Paine, over twenty for James Wyatt. At the height of their career in the 1760s and 70s the Adam brothers had the largest architectural office in the country. Unlike their contemporaries they relied heavily on foreign draughtsmen, Agostino Brunias, Joseph Bonomi, Giuseppe Manocchi, Antonio Zucchi, L-B. Dewez, but not to the exclusion of native talent trained up in the office, such as George Richardson, John Paterson, Richard Crichton and John Charels.

Important architects usually had one key assistant who ran their office, like John Dixon whom Joseph Farington described as 'the artist who is employed by [James] Wyatt to draw for him'. He had joined Wyatt at the very start of his practice and remained there until Wyatt's death in 1813, when he was owed £900 in unpaid wages. For George Dance that role was played by James Peacock who as a result was made assistant Clerk of the Works to the City of London in 1771. In the 1830s George Wightwick was thankful that he had a well-practised surveyor as his chief clerk.[1] But for the bulk of the office work architects' relied on young men who were taken in and trained up over five or seven years. This system of pupillage was the most important development of these decades, bringing a new professionalism to architecture. Previously there had been very few trained architects, rather than builders, surveyors or amateurs who turned to architecture.

PUPILLAGE

William Jones, architect of the Ranelagh rotunda, may have been the first to have called himself an architect rather than a craftsman in the apprenticeship rolls.[2] It is as such that he was described when he took on Jacob Leroux in 1753. By contrast Flitcroft, who was principally an architect by profession, described himself as a joiner. Jones was followed by others before the end of the decade, and both Paine and Chambers are listed as architects. A distinction was made between apprentices and articled pupils, although in practice the difference lay in the premium paid to the architect by articled pupils. Both bound themselves to live and work with a given architect for a number of years, usually five or seven, during which time their board and lodging would be provided and they would be instructed in the 'Art, Profession and Business' of architecture but would not be paid. The distinction was largely one of social status: professional men took articled pupils, craftsmen apprentices. William Jones received a premium of £50 from Leroux, and both Chambers and Paine demanded premiums of £200 once they were

established. Interestingly, Taylor, who is often described as establishing the pattern of the architectural profession, never took premiums but bound his pupils by indenture, according to C.R. Cockerell whose father S.P. Cockerell had trained in his office.[3] The elder Cockerell followed his master in this, and for Charles Tatham the resulting lowly status of an apprentice was too much: he ran away when he discovered his duties included waiting at table.

An anonymous pamphlet published in 1773 and attributed to George Dance, entitled 'An Essay on the Qualifications and Duties of an Architect', shows that despite Taylor and S.P. Cockerell articles had become accepted as the way to become an architect and by 1790 this had become standard, although as yet there were no regulations that demanded it.[4] There were still exceptions like Thomas Cubitt and Decimus Burton who trained in the building trade or Edward Blore and Thomas Rickman who came to architecture through architectural history and the study of medieval buildings, but nearly all the architects illustrated here who began their career after 1790 did so aged about fifteen as a pupil in an architect's office.

The account given by the 1773 pamphlet of the years spent as a pupil shows that the training given to Regency architects had already been established:

'the first Year or two, he [the architect] instructs him how to reduce to Practice those Rules of Arithmetic and Geometry he has learned at School, by applying them to the Mensuration of the several Artificers Works, taking Care at the same Time that he improves himself in his Drawing, and particularly in every Branch of it in relation to Architecture. When about two or three Years are elapsed, the Youth is taught to design, and to draw correctly the Plans, Sections, and Elevations of all Kinds of Edifices; his Master desirous that nothing shall be wanting to complete him, has proper Persons to give him all necessary Instructions in his Absence; and our youth is instructed in Mechanics, Hydraulics and Perspective . . . He is now drawing near the latter Part of the Time he was articled for, and his Master, in order to complete his Education, and form his Taste, takes an Opportunity of either sending or taking him abroad . . . He now returns Home, at the Age of Two or Three and Twenty, after having made the very best Use of his Travels, and in a Time after commences Business for himself, and is by Profession an Architect.'

Pupils lived with their masters, sometimes content, sometimes labouring under the restrictions. Benjamin Ferrey, articled to A.C. Pugin (father of A.W.N.), later recalled the harsh discipline of Mrs Pugin: 'It was severe and restrictive in the extreme, unrelieved by any of the relaxations essential to the healthy education of youth.' Once she had woken at 4 a.m. there was no peace to be had in the house, and all pupils were expected to be at work by 6 a.m: 'A pitiable sight indeed it was to see the shivering youths reluctantly creeping down in the midst of winter to waste their time by a sleepy attempt to work before breakfast [at 8.30].' Breakfast brought no relaxation, no talking was allowed then or at dinner, and pupils worked on until 8 p.m., after which they were allowed a little time to themselves before going to bed at 10 p.m. 'Excellent as was the course of studies pursued in the office, the cold, cheerless, and unvarying round of duty, though enlivened by the cheerful manner and kind attention of the elder Pugin, was wretched and discouraging.'[5] Perhaps it was not surprising that though the office was always full of pupils few ended up as architects.

For some who arrived with romantic visions of architecture reality could come as a shock. 'I had no idea beforehand of the line of practice followed by my future initiator into the mysteries of my profession', wrote George Gilbert Scott who was articled to James Edmeston in 1827.

'I went to him with a mythic veneration for his supposed skill and for his imaginary works, though without an idea of what they might be. The morning after I was deposited at his house, he invited me to walk out and see some of his works — oh, horrors! the bubble burst, and the fond imaginations of my youthful imagination was realized in the form of a few second-rate brick houses, with cemented porticoes of two ungainly columns each! I shall never forget the sudden letting down of my

aspirations. A somewhat romantic youth, assigned to follow the noble art of architecture for the love he had formed for it from the ancient churches of his neighbourhood, condemned to indulge his taste by building houses at Hackney in the debased style of 1827!'[6]

The varied range of a young pupil's activity, the mixture of education and practical experience, is shown by the first months George Basevi spent in Soane's office after he joined in 1810. The primacy of the orders was made clear during the seven trial weeks spent in the office before his articles were signed. These were devoted to drawing the five orders, starting with the mouldings. The Tuscan order received one day, Doric two, Ionic four and he finished with an elaborate Corinthian capital 21 inches by 18 inches on which he spent eleven days. Once he was officially part of the office he was sent with two others to survey a house in Montague Place, before working on the drawings for Dulwich College and spending a day squaring dimensions. This was followed by time drawing temples and beginning perspective. He was then sent to Chelsea Infirmary to take notes of the work in hand and spent five days drawing a view of a room there.[7]

Soane's pupils were lucky: his practice was large and varied, and Soane was committed to training his pupils. George Wightwick, who was apprenticed to Edward Lapidge in 1818, was not so fortunate: 'I expected to find a tutor: I found only an employer.' Lapidge's attitude was summed up in the phrase: 'I will give you the opportunity of learning; but you must teach yourself.' The miscellaneous and unsystematic character of the practice left him uninformed about the full nature of the profession, and as most of Lapidge's practice was in the country he saw little of the building operations except those related to copying working drawings and specifications or mathematical computations of estimates. 'In performing my office duties I learned to write, and to cypher, and to make such working drawings as were necessary for buildings of small pretension.'

Knowledge of architectural detail and the principles of design were left to Wightwick in the occasional intervals of leisure in the office or the evenings. Here he covered quires of paper with designs suitable for Athens or Rome which Lapidge dismissed as 'building palaces by the yard' (although Soane commended the pupil's fantasies in his lectures: 'Nothing can be more useful to the Student than his own theoretical dreams of magnificent compositions produced by warm imagination'[8]). The mundane nature of much of the pupil's work, though a valuable training, had little immediate reward:

'While the young architect rejoices in studying the Greek and Roman orders, his taste rejects, however his duty obeys, the orders of his master to work upon a measuring book full of "cross multiplication", as thus — $12':8'' \times 17':3'' \times 9':4'' = 2039':4''$. Drawing out the combined form of pedestal, column, entablature, and balustrade complete, is a task carrying with it its own reward; but the labours of the "specification" and "estimate" are such as only find their reward at a future period, when knowledge brings practice, practice income, and income the means of following up a love's hopes.'

When Wightwick was in a position to take on pupils he worked hard to ensure that they received a proper architectural education.[9]

A good architect had a profound effect on his pupils. In 1824 Cockerell wrote 'I shall never get entirely out of Smirke's manner in my first works I appealed to Smirke in all things. & nothing but 7 years freedom & travel could ever relieve me from the master's spell.'[10] Smirke, who ran one of the largest and most efficient Regency practices, was particularly influential. The early style and office practice of William Burn, his first pupil, were those of his master.[11] Henry Roberts, who had been a pupil of Charles Fowler, spent some years in Smirke's office: 'whose tastes, habits, modes of construction, and method of making working drawings, he thoroughly imbibed'.[12]

BOOKS

Edmund Aikin, also articled to a respectable but dull surveyor and architect, was another who passed his time in dreaming of more glorious

architecture: 'The glories of his art were never absent from his thoughts; he sketched, he planned, he meditated, and his imagination revelled with delight amid temples, palaces, and triumphal arches of his creation.'[13] Scott found much the same deadening effect in the common routine of building and specifying; his real learning he got from his own reading and drawing — Stuart's *The Antiquities of Athens*, the works of the Dilettanti Society, Vitruvius and such books on Gothic architecture as there were. He taught himself perspective in a fortnight from Joshua Kirby's *Perspective* and, in the summer holidays, sketched medieval buildings near his home and then drew them up in the evenings.[14]

The same books crop up repeatedly in architects' accounts of their education. The chief works in J.B. Papworth's office were the first two volumes of *The Antiquities of Athens*, the three volumes of Peter Nicholson's *An Architectural Dictionary*; Alberti's *Architecture*; Nicholson's *Carpenter's New Guide*; Sir William Chambers's *A Treatise on the Decorative Part of Civil Architecture*; Brook Taylor's *Perspective*; a few small abridgements of Palladio, presumably cheap eighteenth-century editions; and, rather surprisingly, Batty Langley's *Gothic Architecture Improved*.[15] The volumes of Chambers and Stuart bore traces of use by Papworth's pupils and friends.

The three key authors were Stuart, Chambers and Nicholson. The first volume of *The Antiquities of Athens* was published in 1762, but its greatest influence was during the Regency when subsequent volumes were published in 1789, 1795 and 1816. Chambers had published the first part of his *Treatise on Civil Architecture* in 1759. Despite a second edition in 1768 and a 'considerably augmented' third edition in 1791 the intended second part of the book was never published, and in 1791 it was renamed *A Treatise on the Decorative Part of Civil Architecture*. It became the standard work on the orders and further editions by Joseph Gwilt and J.B. Papworth were published in 1824 and 1825. Wightwick considered it the best introduction to architecture for a young architect and indeed Barry's early notebooks were a mixture of lists of prices, calculations of dimensions and methods of

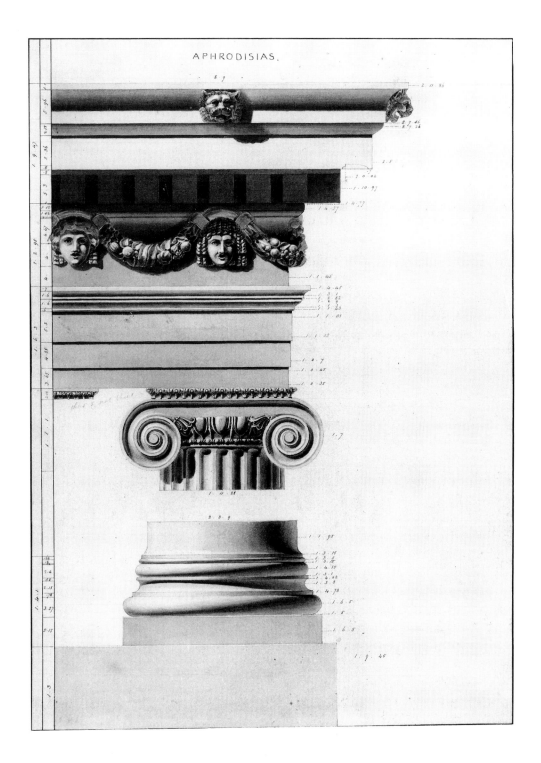

Fig.1 **Francis Octavius Bedford 1784-1858** and **John Peter Gandy 1787-1850**
Order of the columns of the exterior portico of the Agora at Aphrodisias, Greece
Measured drawing for the engraver, 1817. Pen and sepia wash (380 × 280)

measuring and valuation together with studies from Chambers. Both Tatham and Scott taught themselves to draw from it.[16] Nicholson was a prolific architectural writer, but his most important work was his *An Architectural Dictionary* first published in 1819, which Scott referred to as 'our office text book'.[17]

Leading architects had extensive collections of architectural books; Soane's still exists, those of George Dance and Robert Smirke can be gauged from the catalogues of the sales held after their deaths. Young architects and Academicians could also use the library of the Royal Academy, something of which J.B. Papworth certainly availed himself, although there were complaints in 1817 that students did not have sufficient access to the library.

The Regency saw a great advance in architectural publishing. Innumerable aspiring architects published pattern books in the vain hope of attracting the public's attention. Many architects like Wightwick, Papworth and Aikin turned their hand to architectural journalism, publishing both books and articles. All were aware of the importance of their buildings getting the right publicity: Mr Michel advised Charles Cockerell that he should 'publish an exposé of the motives of the design of my new chapel [the Hanover Chapel, Regent Street] because otherwise these things are often mistaken, get an ill name ill founded — or may be totally overlooked'.[18]

There was continued interest in the remains of classical Greece from the Dilettanti Society who published further volumes of the series begun by Stuart, including the *Unedited Antiquities of Attica* in 1817 (Fig. 1). But even more important was the new interest in analysing and publishing the antiquities of Britain. A.C. Pugin, encouraged by John Nash who felt that there was a want of practical books on Gothic architecture, turned from architectural draughtsmanship to the publication of books on medieval architecture in partnership with writers and publishers such as Ackermann, Britton and Brayley. John Carter, whose knowledge of medieval example was put to good use in his unpublished illustrations for Horace Walpole's *Castle of Otranto* (Fig. 2), published *The Ancient*

Architecture of England in 1795-1814, an attempt to set out 'in a regular manner' the 'Orders of architecture during the British, Roman, Saxon, and Norman Aeras'. Much more significant was the publication in 1817 of Thomas Rickman's *An Attempt to Discriminate the Styles of English Architecture from the Conquest to the Reformation* (Fig. 3), the first systematic treatise on Gothic architecture in England. Never was the relationship between architecture and architectural publishing closer.

DRAWING LESSONS

John Soane in his lectures to the Royal Academy stressed the importance of the student gaining facility in drawing: 'He must be familiar with the use of the Pencil and must not be satisfied with Geometrical delineations, for the real effect of a Composition can only be correctly shown by Perspective representations. The student must therefore be fully acquainted with the theory and practice of Perspective, and be able to sketch his ideas with facility and correctness.'[19]

Although practical experience in drawing could be found in the office, most pupils sought extra tuition from specific drawing masters like Thomas Malton, Richard Brown 'Architect and Professor of Perspective' or George Maddox, 'a man of real ability with wonderful power of drawing and high appreciation' (Fig. 4), who taught Scott. Scott always regretted that he put off taking lessons until his last year of pupillage to avoid burdening his father.[20] Maddox had many pupils, among them Decimus Burton.

George Taylor, who was articled to Joseph Parkinson in 1804, recalled how he used to get up at 3 a.m. and walk to Highgate with his fellow-pupil Edward Cresy to take lessons in oil painting, returning in time for breakfast.[21] John Dobson showed similar dedication. He had been born in Newcastle and was articled to the leading master builder in the city, David Stephenson, in 1803. At the same time he took lessons in perspective from an Italian refugee, Boniface Musso. But this did not satisfy him, and in 1810 he came to London to take instruction from the leading watercolourist, John Varley. Varley was impressed by his ability and

Fig.2 **John Carter 1748-1817**
Design for 'The Entry of Frederick into the Castle of Otranto' from Horace Walpole's
The Castle of Otranto, 1790
Pen and watercolour (590 × 490)

offered to teach him if he came at 5 a.m., which he did.

ROYAL ACADEMY

Education was not left entirely to the young architect and his master. The Royal Academy had been founded in 1768 to improve the quality of the arts, including architecture. It offered a regular course of lectures in architecture and in perspective, together with use of the library. Architects were also allowed into the studios where painters and sculptors drew from life and from casts and benefited from the criticism of Academicians who volunteered their services as visitors. Competitions were held annually on a given theme for which gold and silver medals were awarded. For many successful architects such as Soane this was the first step in their career.

Entry to the Royal Academy schools was competitive, applicants had to provide a portfolio of designs such as the plans, elevations and sections of a theatre which J.B. Papworth submitted — C.J. Richardson petitioned Soane for time off to prepare his portfolio in 1826. This examination was no formality. Wightwick failed. Although many students attended whilst in articles, other students had completed them and were working as a clerk or assistant; Papworth was twenty-three. Scott, however, never got round to applying.

The Royal Academy also had a specific room for architectural drawings in the annual exhibition to which aspirant as well as practising architects were encouraged to submit designs, measured drawings and ideal schemes. Charles Barry's list of entries as a pupil between 1812 and 1815 are typical of the subjects exhibited: the Interior of Westminster Hall, a Design for a Hall, for a Museum and Library and for a Building in a Nobleman's Park.[22]

The lectures on architecture were the only public teaching to be had on the theory of the profession. The first Professor of Architecture was Thomas Sandby, who delivered a series of six lectures every year from 1770 until two years before his death in 1798, when they were read for him. He was succeeded by George Dance, who failed to produce any lectures and was replaced by Soane in 1806.

Soane took infinite trouble over his lectures, which were first delivered in 1809 and continued, despite a temporary suspension, until the year before his death. Both Sandby's and Soane's lectures had a profound impact and Soane himself recalled the 'powerful impression the sight of that beautiful work produced on myself and on many young artists of those days' as Sandby's vast drawing of a Bridge of Magnificence was unfolded across the lecture room.[23]

The lectures were not without controversy and T.L. Donaldson's obituary of Soane summed up his initial success and later decline:

'Yet it must be confessed that, at the period, his lectures produced considerable effect. They directed the attention of the student to the pure example of ancient and modern times; they inculcated a high tone of morals in professional practice; and they excited in the breast of the young architect, a glow and ambition for distinction. But when these lectures at a later period, although extended by an additional series, came to be repeated; and the later researches of subsequent travellers, and the improved acquaintance, which we had acquired in other styles of art and particularly in Gothic, were overlooked; and when the Professor did not advance the progress of the age; the repetition became wearisome, and failed of exciting the attention which they formerly commanded. The numerous attendance, therefore, of visitors and students, attracted in the first instance by the novelty of the subject and by the prodigious number, variety, and beauty of the drawings, gradually dwindled away, and the chair of Professor of Architecture, at the Royal Academy, became a title without those results to the art, which it ought to produce.'[24]

PRACTICAL EXPERIENCE

Education, both public and private, and training in the office was mixed with experience on the building site. By the end of their time pupils were often allowed to act as clerk of works. Scott benefited greatly when Edmeston allowed him and Enoch Springbett to act as joint clerk of works on a school he was building at the end of Scott's

Fig.3 **Thomas Rickman 1776-1841**
Design for the frontispiece of *An Attempt to Discriminate the Styles of*
English Architecture from the Conquest to the Reformation, c. 1817
Pen and wash (220 × 150)

pupillage.[25] Many young architects took this further, either taking lessons in surveying during pupillage like John Dobson who went to Mr Hall of Stamfordham while still articled to David Stephenson or spending time with a firm of surveyors or builders after finishing pupillage.

Scott was advised by a surveyor, Mr Waller, to spend time with a builder and Waller provided an introduction to Messrs Peto and Grissell, who were then working on Charles Fowler's Hungerford Market (130-2). This was on a scale far greater than any Scott had experienced and introduced him to innovative building materials. He subsequently praised Fowler's working drawings as being among the best he ever saw. He was also able to borrow

and copy specifications by different architects. He did not stay long: Peto did not relish the way he pried so closely into the basis of the prices of work and materials. But Scott considered his time here invaluable, giving him insight into every description of practical work.[26]

TRAVEL

Travel had become a key part in the young architect's training in the middle of the eighteenth century. 'Travelling to an Artist is the last Stage of a regular Education,' declared Chambers, and most of the leading architects of the second half of the century trained in Rome. 'The use of an Architect who travels,' declared Gandy, 'is to pick with

Fig.4 **George Maddox 1760-1843**
Classical composition, *c.* 1815. Pen (120 × 200)

judgement and taste from those places he sees the best flowers (to speak in allegory) from every garden the Ancients have left us, and to select them in the mind that they may always be as a mould either to improve upon or follow.'[27]

Detailed study of the best monuments of ancient Rome and Greece still formed the core of the visiting architect's activities. 'The ladders are brought, and I am mounting, and scrambling and measuring the temple to prove the measurements of others. Well: at all events they are near enough for any practical purpose' wrote George Wightwick of his survey of the Temple of Vesta at Tivoli. Two months were spent in Florence. Four were all he could spend in Rome: 'My four months stay is completed. My portfolio is filled with drawings, sketches, and accurately measured delineations of many an antique from the Vatican Galleries, but my purse is fearfully diminishing. I dare not venture further southward.' After a month in Venice he stopped off in Vicenza where 'I could live and die!' and then headed back to England.[28] Wightwick's trip was unusually hurried, most young architects spent several years.

Thomas Hope's sketches of the Villa Poniatowski (Fig. 5) and Tatham's copy of a Spanish architect's survey of the roof timbers of San Paolo fuori le Mure in Rome (Fig. 6) show that architects abroad studied more than just antiquities. Nor was it only practical information that Tatham and his fellows sought.

Fig.5 Thomas Hope 1769-1831
Studies in the garden of the Villa Poniatowski, Rome
Leaf from a sketchbook, 1812. Pen (100 × 160)

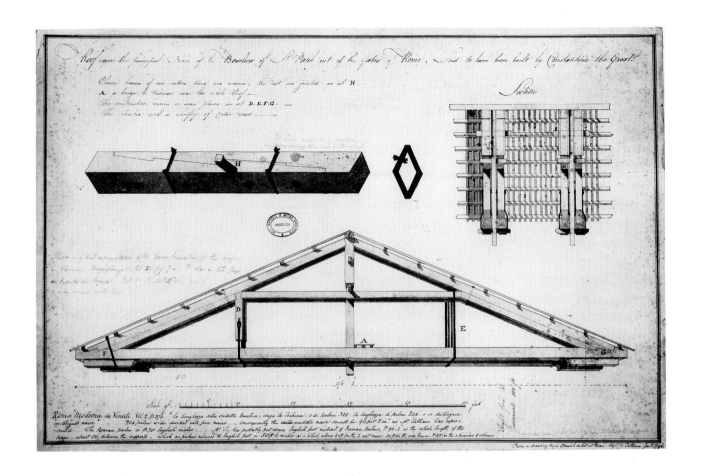

Fig.6 **Charles Heathcote Tatham 1772-1842**
Record drawing of the Basilica of San Paolo fuori le Mure, Rome
Section of roof and details of joinery, 1796
Pen with sepia, buff and grey washes (350 × 530)

Signs of recognition, like the two medals given to Thomas Harrison by Pope Clement IV in 1773, could be useful proof of their ability when they returned to England. Such marks of esteem did not always live up to their face value. Tatham brought back a diploma which he displayed on his wall, but according to Farington he had received it by letter having sent a suitable fee to an engraver in Bologna.[29]

The early 1790s saw several significant young architects in Rome, including James Playfair (Fig. 7), who returned to Scotland in 1793, but the French invasion in 1797 forced those who remained to flee. Sensibly, Tatham left when the invasion was imminent, but Joseph Gandy only escaped thanks to a King's Messenger who knew his family. For most of the next twenty years Rome was closed to the English. A few architects like William Wilkins and Charles Cockerell cast beyond Rome to Turkey and Greece, where

Cockerell made his name discovering the Aegina Marbles in 1811. Robert Smirke contemplated visiting Paris in 1801 disguised as an American, but put off his visit until the brief Peace of Amiens, after which he travelled through Italy to Sicily and on to Greece.

But these were exceptional. A generation of architects were cut off from their traditional links with Rome. One result was that architects were forced to look more to Britain at a time when touring their own country was becoming popular with the middle classes, increasing an appreciation of English architecture that was already becoming evident. Scott spent his summer holidays as a pupil sketching around his home, and on leaving his pupillage spent several months touring England.[30] Dobson always made sketches when travelling,[31] and Rickman's timebooks in the British Library are often interrupted by a rapid sketch. The practice was pragmatic, as Gandy showed when he wrote to Soane in 1816, 'The road from York to Lancaster through Wensleydale is picturesque, and not without old castles and churches in the towns, which the eye of the architect ought not to miss noting, if he collects for the future.'[32] Carefully annotated drawings of medieval details (Fig. 8) provided a useful source for J.A. Repton when making Gothic designs.

With the ending of war with France the floodgates opened. When George Taylor was in Rome as part of the three years he spent in Italy and Greece with Edward Cresy from 1817 to 1820 fellow-students included John Sanders, William Purser, Philip Hardwick, T.L. Donaldson, Lewis Vulliamy, George Basevi, John Goldicutt and John Soane junior.[33] Other architects on the Continent whom he did not come across included Charles Barry, William Kinnaird and George Scott. From Rome many of them went on to Greece and some, like Barry and Henry Parke, to Egypt (Fig. 9).

Financing such a trip was always difficult. Soane had been lucky enough to receive a travel scholarship from the Royal Academy, as did Vulliamy, but there were few of these. Holland allowed Tatham £60 a year for three years. Scott relied on a small legacy from his father, while Wightwick was lent money by his stepfather on the security of his father's legacy. Rather better-off were the sons of indulgent fathers like Cockerell and Soane junior, while Cockerell recommended Nash to allow James Pennethorne (in whom he took a particular interest) £250 a year.[34] For good draughtsmen like J.P. Gandy, the best solution was a commission from the Dilettanti Society to provide illustrations for one of their books (Fig. 1).

ESTABLISHING A PRACTICE

A successful, well-publicised trip to Rome or the Near East could do wonders for establishing a reputation as C.R. Cockerell found, but whether a young architect had travelled abroad or not there still remained the difficulty of establishing an independent practice. Many were slow in taking the plunge. Henry Seward worked for about five years as an assistant in Soane's office after completing his articles before setting himself up in partnership with George Byfield, Surveyor to the Dean and Chapter of Westminster and twenty years his senior. Francis Edwards entered Soane's office as an improver when he was twenty-two, left that to work four days a week for Seward at twenty-six, and only found independence aged thirty-nine when Seward was appointed Assistant Surveyor-General and gave up private practice, handing him the commission for St John the Baptist in Hoxton.

A period as an assistant could prove valuable experience as Scott found when he entered the office of Henry Roberts after he had won the Fishmongers' Hall competition in 1832. 'I was the only clerk in the office at the time, though he subsequently took a pupil, so that I had the advantage of making all the working drawings of this considerable public building, from the foundation to the finish; and of helping in measuring up the extras and occasions, as well as of constantly seeing the work during its progress.'[35] Drawing up designs was the staple of the assistant — Thomas Taylor who was in James Wyatt's office for eight years 'was in the Habit of making Plans, Elevations, and Sections of some of the most distinguished Buildings in the Kingdom' — but for those with more flair there was a chance of greater responsibility. Tatham 'was employed to *design* and draw *at large* all the ornamental decorations' for Henry

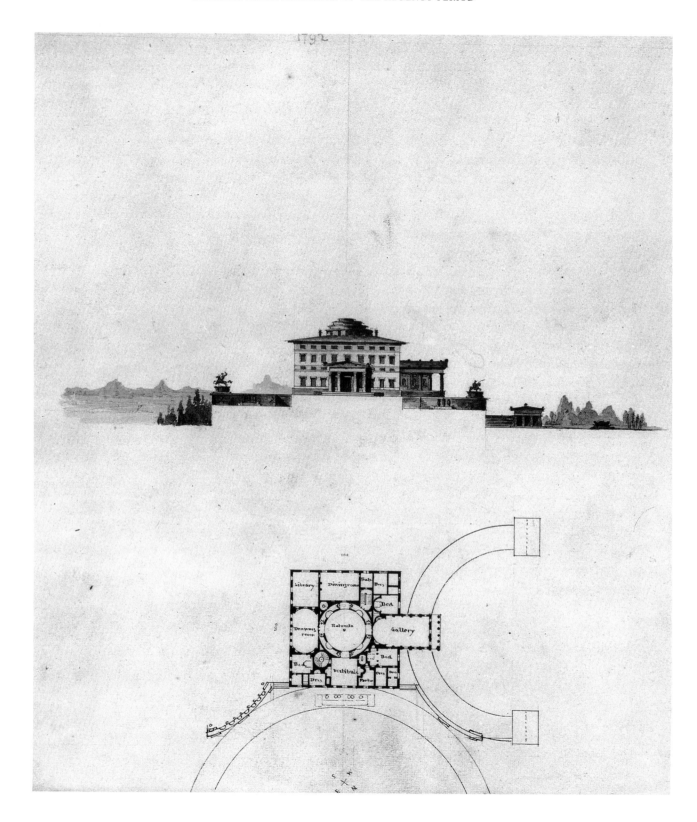

Fig.7 **James Playfair 1755-1794**
Design for an Italianate villa. Plan and elevation, 1792
Pen and watercolour (260 × 350)

Holland's Drury Lane Theatre.[36] G.S. Repton's letters to John Harford over Blaise Hamlet in 1810 are particularly revealing, showing that he would receive sketches of the proposed cottages from Nash (who was then in Ireland) and would then draw them up or turn them into working drawings before sending them on to Harford.[37]

George Wightwick wittily described the tribulations of trying to establish himself. He had been unable to gain a place at the Royal Academy schools, and for a time continued to work for Lapidge after completing his articles in 1823, while also making topographical drawings for Britton and Pugin's *Public Buildings of London.* His trip to Italy in 1825 was a simple investment rather than part of a broad education, but on his return he found it no easier to get work. Kindly receptions, good reports from John Britton and praise for his Italian sketches all ended with the same response that there was 'no need for assistance at present'. Failing to find regular work he served for a time as Soane's secretary on a salary of £80 a year (he had asked for £100), writing out his defence of the law courts at Westminster and reading him *Gil Blas.* But, fed up with working six and a half days a week and with Soane's irritability, he handed in his notice.

Since work still eluded him, a friend offered him a loan of £300 to establish himself and gave him some advice:

'Engage, instantly, apartments of a respectable official character in a good, professional locality. Put a brass plate on your door, announcing "Mr W-ARCHITECT." Get your views of the Roman Ruins handsomely mounted; obtain an estimate for having them well lithographed, and for the printing of a suitable accompanying letter-press. Let one lithograph be immediately prepared, and have something more than the full number of required impressions taken. By showing the drawings and the sample print, obtain as many subscribers as you can from the profession and other influential persons. So much of your time as remains unoccupied by conducting the publication of your pictorial work, and in filling your subscription list, you will of course give to (at least apparent) professional work in your office. Seek work — and, if you cannot obtain it, *make* work. Let those who come to see your Roman Views and to enter their names as subscribers, find you occupied upon plans for things, — you know what: town-halls, and churches, and literary institutions, and national academies. Look out for advertisements "to architects:" try for premiums, and never mind not obtaining them; meanwhile, I'll venture to predict your work's subscription list will support you, and if it do not, something else will, depend upon it!'

The advice was duly taken. A ground-floor room was taken in the Adelphi with a garret above in which to sleep. *Select View of Roman Antiquities* was published in 1827, making a modest profit but bringing no commissions. A couple of competitions were unsuccessfully entered. A fire-damaged house was surveyed and a porch designed, but no proper architectural work came. In his boredom he wrote a play and a volume of essays entitled *The Life and Remains of Wilmot Warwick* which was described by *The Examiner* as good enough for 'lassitude and a sofa'. Finally, despairing of establishing himself in London he moved to Plymouth where connections with one of the leading families provided valuable introductions. He was taken into partnership by John Foulston, flourished, and was soon averaging £1,000 a year.[38]

Even those who were subsequently immensely successful like Charles Barry could find it difficult to get started. When he returned to England in 1820 he competed fruitlessly in public competitions and at times even considered settling in a provincial town. Luckily he received much encouragement and substantial support from the firm of Middleton and Bailey, essentially surveyors, to whom he had been articled.[39] Some just gave up. George Mitchell went off and became a sugar planter in Tobago. John Leach, who was a contemporary of S.P. Cockerell in Taylor's office, turned to law and became Master of the Rolls. Richard Jones, son of 'an eminent architect and surveyor' was forced to earn a living on the stage by an unfortunate speculation of his father's; as did C.J. Mathews, a pupil of A.C. Pugin's and subsequently one of the most celebrated Victorian comedians.

*

COMPETITIONS

Publishing a book like Wightwick, whether a record of foreign travels or a pattern book of proposed designs like Joseph Gandy's *The Rural Architect* and *Designs for Cottages* of 1805, was one way of trying to draw attention to yourself, but as Wightwick and Gandy found it was seldom enough.

For the struggling architect there were two key ways to establish a practice. The first was to win a public competition, which generally ensured a commission and meant that the architect was drawn to the attention of the public. This was what happened to Henry Roberts when he won the Fishmongers' Hall competition in 1832. Winning the competition for the Wellington Rooms in 1814 induced Edmund Aikin to settle in Liverpool, although ill-health brought an early end to his career.

It was not only struggling architects who entered. Despite his reservations about competitions Thomas Rickman, then heading one of the most distinguished practices in the country, submitted three entries for the Fitzwilliam Museum competition in 1834 (15-16). But many architects, such as Charles Cockerell, had doubts about competitions, which were easily open to influence and some, like Burn, refused to enter them.

J.B. Papworth was one who did enter competitions in the hope of gaining the large commission that always evaded him. He submitted plans for the General Post Office competition (1819): 'The Designs to consist of Plans, Geometrical Elevations, and Sections to be drawn to a scale of 12 feet to an Inch. Each Design to be distinguished by a number or motto'.[40] Eighty-nine architects submitted designs, and the contract was awarded to Robert Smirke. Eighty-three entries were submitted for the Fishmongers' Hall competition in 1832; thirty-six designs by twenty-seven architects were made for the Fitzwilliam. It was to avoid the problem of dealing with such numbers that the competition for the Royal Manchester Institution in 1824 was restricted to six selected 'Architects of eminence'. The regulations were precise: 'The Plans, Elevations, and Sections to be upon a Scale of 3/16ths of an inch, the Plans and Geometrical Drawings to be

tinted with Indian Ink, without backgrounds, and to be sent in with Motto with the name of the Author sealed up, addressed to the Honorary Secretary.'[41]

SURVEYORSHIP

The other way for a young architect to establish himself was to gain a surveyorship which guaranteed a regular income from which to launch a private practice.

George Basevi was made Surveyor to the newly formed Guardian Assurance Company in 1821, the year after he returned from Italy, and followed this with surveyorships to the Smith's Charity Estate in Brompton in 1829 and to the adjoining Thurloe Estate. For Francis Edwards appointment as Surveyor of the Imperial Gas Company in 1823 was probably vital in setting up his practice. Some architects like Henry Bassett or George Gutch largely restricted their work to surveying, despite the promise of their early careers. George Taylor was happy to give up an unsuccessful attempt to establish a private practice and take up the post of Surveyor of Buildings to the Admiralty in 1824.

Taylor subsequently lost his post when the Admiralty was reorganised, but others found surveying a profitable career. Joseph Gwilt was Surveyor to the Commissioners of Sewers for Surrey, to the Grocers' and Waxchandlers' Companies and to the Imperial Fire Assurance Company. S.P. Cockerell's successful career was laid on the foundation of a battery of such posts: District Surveyor for the parish of St George's, Hanover Square, Inspector of Repairs to the Admiralty, Surveyor of the Foundling and Pulteney Estates, of the East India Company, to the Victualling Office, the sees of Canterbury and London as well as Surveyor of St Paul's Cathedral. According to James Noble the St Katharine's Dock Company arranged to provide their surveyor, George Aitchison, appointed in 1827, with an office and clerk and a salary of £500 for preparatory work, together with 1¾% on the estimated £700,000 to be spent which was expected for three to four years to earn him £3,000 a year.[42]

Aitchison was also architect to the Founders' Company and to the London and Birmingham Railway Company and was said to have been equally competent as architect, engineer and surveyor, 'not only excellent at arrangement and construction, but one of the most beautiful draughtsmen of his day'. This was typical of a time when the distinction between architects and engineers was only beginning to emerge. James Smeaton (1724-92) had been the first to call himself a civil engineer and had been responsible for founding the Society of Civil Engineers in 1771, but several Regency architects, including Daniel Alexander and Charles Busby, called themselves architect-engineers. Thomas Telford, one of the greatest engineers of the day, began as an architect. Smirke was distinguished for his engineering achievement, being an innovator in the use of concrete for foundations, cast-iron for beams, girders and braces, and wrought-iron for ties, beams, joists and supports. Nevertheless, the foundation of the Institute of Civil Engineers in 1818 showed that engineering was developing into a separate profession.

Architects also surveyed buildings on an individual basis, and much of their time was taken up mundanely but profitably 'in the matter of Valuations of Property, and of Dilapidations, as well as Arbitration Cases'.[43] Surveying remained important even for architects as successful as Nash, but the Regency also saw the development of the quantity surveyor as a profession separate from that of the architect. In 1798 Soane was approached by a G. Scott who wished 'to undertake the measuring and valuing of the whole of the Works that come under Your direction . . . This system is now begun to be executed in a certain degree, but not to the extent to which it might be carried.'[44] By the time of Soane's death, thanks to the example he and architects like Smirke set, it was widespread.

A ruthless ability to exploit friends and connections was essential for a young architect. Scott set up his own practice when his father died in 1835 relying on people who had known his father to obtain the appointment of surveyor to the various new workhouse unions around where he lived.[45] Charles Cockerell must have owed his first major commission, for the Hanover Chapel in Regent Street, to his father who was Surveyor to the parish of St

George's, Hanover Square, in which it fell. Robert Smirke quickly established himself in 1805 at the age of twenty-five thanks to the contacts his father, a talented painter and prominent figure in the Royal Academy, could provide. His first major job, designing Lowther Castle, Cumbria, one of the largest houses of the Regency, for the Earl of Lonsdale, was passed on to him in 1806 by another Royal Academician, George Dance, who had too much work to take on a remote house. Friendship with Charles Kemble gained him the building that first made his name, the Covent Garden Theatre of 1808-9. His contacts among the Tories assured him the Royal Mint on the death of James Johnson in 1807 (9-11). He continued to maintain his connections. At least twenty of his patrons were founder members of the Carlton Club which he built in 1833-6.[46]

The only young architect whose career took off as rapidly as Smirke's was Decimus Burton. His father, the builder James Burton, was largely responsible for the success of Regent Street, so it was not surprising that Nash allowed him to design Cornwall and Clarence Terraces in Regent's Park. His first public building on setting up on his own at the age of twenty-three in 1823 was the great colosseum in Regent's Park, his second the screen at Hyde Park Corner, the new ceremonial entrance to London.

Even when an architect did manage to set up a practice disaster always hovered nearby. For Edward Welch and Joseph Hansom winning the competition for Birmingham Town Hall in 1830 should have been the start of a successful practice but they foolishly stood surety for the contractors and were bankrupted. Thomas Sandys was forced to retire when the Durham magistrates for whom he was building a new gaol and county courts had damages of £20,000 awarded against him as the work proved to be fraudulently done and had to be taken down. David Laing left the profession when part of the facade of the Custom House collapsed in 1825 because the beech piling of the foundations proved inadequate. Joseph Woods gave up after a miscalculation of the strength of the iron trusses at the London Commercial Sale Rooms of 1811-12 meant the floor failed and Woods was forced to

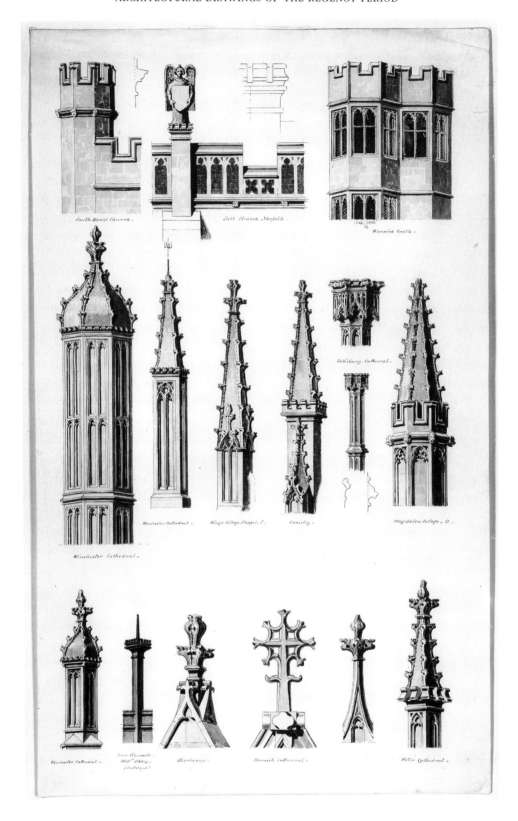

Fig.8 **John Adey Repton 1775-1860**
Sheet of measured drawings of medieval crockets and terminations, n.d.
Pen and wash (470 × 290)

make good at his own expense.

For many ambitious architects, success meant a practice in London, but as Rickman showed first in Liverpool and then in Birmingham, it was possible to be a national architect without being based in London. The Regency was the high point of the major provincial practice, before the railway made every point of the country accessible from London in a way that the stagecoach never could. When John Dobson came to London the painter Robert Smirke, father of the architect, tried to persuade him to set up in the capital. He would probably have prospered had he done so, but he was right to return to Newcastle, for the early years of the nineteenth century were boom years for the North-East. He did not find it easy to establish himself as an architect rather than as a master builder like Stephenson, as his daughter related: 'although he was (with the exception of Mr Bonomi of Durham) the only professional architect between Edinburgh and York, he soon discovered that the demand for his services had to be created. He found that it was easier to profess an art than practise it. An architect's advice was in but little request, and to one so young and unknown engagements came but slowly.' But come they did through hard work and professionalism. According to his daughter 'Mr Dobson, during his long and varied practice, never exceeded an estimate, and never had a legal dispute with a contractor.'[47]

DRAWING OFFICES

For most Regency architects home and office were the same, although that might vary from the aspirant George Wightwick's single rented room with a garret to sleep in to John Nash's great mansion on Lower Regent Street with an eight-room office on the ground floor and seventy-foot long gallery above. George Dance had two offices, one in the Office of Works at the Guildhall from where he operated as Clerk of the City Works, and another, smaller office at home, from where he carried out his small private practice.

Some successful architects were able to move to new houses as their practices flourished, leaving their offices in their old house. S.P. Cockerell had his office in Old Burlington Street but lived in a suburban villa at Westbourne Green. However, when his son set up practice he shared his father's office and lived above. Success meant that he later moved to Eaton Square in 1830. Samuel Wyatt left his office in Berwick Street when he moved to Albion Mill in 1798, although he moved the office to Surrey Street off the Strand in 1803. But Jeffry Wyatville never moved from his relatively small house at 49 Lower Brook Street, while Soane kept his office in Lincoln's Inn Fields.

Working conditions varied. John Britton provided his four pupils with a pleasant and comfortable drawing office in his garden, a rarity in London. C.R. Cockerell may also have had his drawing office in his garden. Nash's drawing office at 29 Dover Street, his first London house, occupied in 1798, had a writing office on the top floor, connected to his study by a back stair, with a large tripartite north-facing window. Wyatville added a wing in the garden of his Lower Brook Street house creating a large drawing office on the ground floor and a dignified gallery above. George Taylor started off his career by renting 52 Bedford Square, letting the stabling and using the large back offices as his office. Soane had a two-storey drawing office at the rear of his house.

HOURS

While contacts could help an architect on his way, it was hard work and efficiency that were usually responsible for his success. The example of Sir Robert Taylor, who was worth £180,000 when he died, was ever before aspiring architects. George Byfield, a pupil of Taylor's, told Farington that 'Sir Robert Taylor had three rules for growing rich viz: rising early, keeping appointments and regular accounts.' John Nash, another pupil, told Farington that Taylor went to bed at 8 or 9 p.m. and rose at 3 a.m., calling his pupils at 5. According to Horace Walpole he always travelled overnight.[48]

Long hours and the ability to sleep in coaches were frequently the mark of the successful Regency architect. Given the rapid improvement in roads and coaching systems at this time such an architect could cover remarkable distances and keep up a practice all over the country. Nash told Farington that he travelled eleven thousand miles in a year.[49]

Thomas Rickman could spend two nights out of three travelling without ill-effect, and G.G. Scott recalled how in the hectic period when he was trying to establish a practice he spent weeks on horseback canvassing newly formed workhouse unions alternating with periods of close hard work in his little office in Carlton Chambers and coach rides, chiefly at night, to attend the meetings of

Always before them, too, was the prospect of James Wyatt who despite the most successful practice of his day died in severe financial embarrassment.

NUMBER OF CLERKS

As well as his sons and several pupils, James Wyatt had four clerks working under Dixon. The staff at

Fig.9 **Henry Parke ?1792-1835**
View of the temple at El Sibaiya, Egypt, 1823-4
Pencil (345 × 475)

guardians. John Dobson rose at 4 or 5 a.m. and if necessary could work constantly until 12 p.m. Charles Barry seldom rose later than 6 a.m. and often was up at 4 or 5 a.m. Papworth, for one, seldom took a holiday.[50]

Long though the hours were, they were not extraordinary. Soane initially worked his pupils from 7 a.m. to 7 p.m. in summer and 8 a.m. to 8 p.m. in winter, although in 1810 this changed to 9 a.m. to 8 p.m.[51] Sunday was the only day of rest. By comparison the hours of the London surveyor and architect Michael Searles seem modest, from 9 a.m. to 6 p.m.[52]

Dance's Office of Works in the Guildhall fluctuated between five and ten in the 1790s, all paid directly by Dance. Ten was a good size for a successful practice; that was the number Wyatville had in 1812 according to Farington. On average Soane had between four and six articled pupils, one paid assistant, a surveyor and several clerks of works. By contrast Charles Cockerell never had a large office. He was too much of an individualist and perfectionist to want one.[53]

A good clerk or assistant could command about £80 to £100. In Soane's office G.A. Underwood, who worked as an assistant in 1815, received £100.

Joseph Blandford, a clerk from 1795-7, £80. Francis Edwards, who had little experience having been apprenticed to a cabinet-maker but showed a strong talent for architectural drawing, entered the office as an improver on £40 in 1806, rising to £60 in 1809 and £100 in 1810 as he became increasingly valuable. In 1791 Robert Woodgate was negotiating with Soane to supervise all his work in Ireland on £100 a year, including board, lodging and travelling expenses.[54]

Charles Cockerell paid his chief assistant James Noble, a draughtsman rather than a designer, £250 in 1826. This was slightly more than he had made himself; after expenses, Cockerell's average income in 1817-25 was £236 8s.[55] According to Farington, G.S. Repton earned £1,500 a year while in Nash's office, but his position was exceptional.[56]

DESIGN PRACTICE

Once an architect had been approached to make a design his first act was to visit the proposed site. Margaret Dobson recalled how John Dobson went about designing houses:

'When he was engaged to design a building of any importance, it was his invariable custom on paying a preliminary visit to the proposed site, to carefully inspect the locality, and make himself thoroughly acquainted with the *genus loci* from every point of view. Then, having thoroughly imbued his mind with the true spirit of the place he would, with unerring precision, choose the exact spot where the building should stand. This done, Mr Dobson would then make his design, also a perspective drawing at the same time. Thus it was that the works of this architect always harmonise so remarkably with their surroundings, of which they seem at once to form a part'[57]

Site visits were not only concerned with the setting. Rickman's timebooks and office diaries show that he was always concerned to check the possible foundations and establish local sources of key materials like stone. On his first visit to Oulton near Leeds (97-99) he sketched out a proposed design for the new church and roughed out a provisional estimate which he showed to the Blayds family before leaving. Once back in the office he elaborated on the sketches before leaving them to his partner Henry Hutchinson to draw up neatly. These were then sent off to the Blaydses who approved them subject to only minor changes.

The church at Oulton was designed with remarkably little fuss. Soane's commissions usually involved more toing and froing which can be followed in detail because his office records survive almost in their entirety in the Soane Museum. As well as the drawings there are his daybooks, which record the daily tasks of each member of the office, and his account journals which record all payments made through the office. The only things missing are his letters. There are three brief letter books, but Soane does not seem to have kept copies of his letters consistently. Soane first visited the site at Tyringham in Buckinghamshire, one of his most successful commissions, in August 1792. He next sent his pupil Frederick Meyer to make a detailed survey of the existing house which was drawn up in full on his return. After proposals to remodel the house were rejected Soane worked up a series of alternative schemes which were shown to the owner William Praed in September 1793. Soane's initial sketches would have been redrawn by his office and then checked over and possibly altered by him before being sent to the client. (After the 1780s Soane rarely produced finished designs himself.) Once Praed had settled on one scheme this would be further worked on before a final presentation set of drawings was delivered. In April 1795 the office was at work on the working drawings for the carcase of the house, and in 1796 Soane was designing the interior. Papworth's drawings for remodelling Little Grove, Barnet, London, follow a similar pattern; although no preliminary sketches survive, the sequence begins with the contract drawings (65-71).[58]

Wyatville ran a carefully controlled practice, having seen in his uncle's office the havoc that inefficiency could cause, and the evolution of Dinton Park, Wiltshire, from sketches drawn on site to the final working drawings can be traced through the seventy-five surviving drawings in the RIBA (32-9). A notebook at Chatsworth shows how Wyatville would record the existing building in detail, noting down possible ideas for improvement. When alternative designs were sufficiently advanced for submission they were fully drawn out, rendered in watercolour and sometimes mounted in a leather-bound volume with a title page and list of contents. Designs were produced without delay. Within two months of visiting Chatsworth he had produced sketch plans, and final presentation drawings were presented within six months. At Banner Cross in Yorkshire, where General Murray was impatient to start, Wyatville was first consulted in July 1817, sketches and then plans were sent the following month, and the building was set out in September. Rickman was equally fast. It was less than two months between his first receiving a letter from John Blayds and the final design for the church at Oulton being approved.

Wyatville abandoned James Wyatt's practice of drawings being made on site (although at Soane's Tyringham some of the drawings were made by the clerk of works). All drawings were prepared in the office, checked by him and signed before despatch. His claim that he gave his contractors 'precise drawings' is borne out by the large numbers in which drawings from his office survive. For relatively small alterations at Towneley Hall, Lancashire, essentially two rooms, there are thirty-two drawings. The RIBA has 423 drawings for Ashridge Park, Hertfordshire.[59] Smirke's vast practice was founded on a similar reputation for efficiency and thoroughness which he passed on to his pupils. T.L. Donaldson's obituary of William Burn recorded that 'He sketched with great accuracy and neatness, and following the example of his master Sir Robert Smirke, he in his earliest works at least drew out the plans with the minutest accuracy, dimensioning with his own hand every part and detail with peculiar clearness, so as to afford no excuse to the builder for any mistakes or blunders.'[60] This is borne out by his contract drawings for the Greenock Custom House and Excise Office (7-8) and for the Crichton Royal Institution (12-14).

Given enough drawings it is easy to follow the design process from inception to completion but descriptions of how architects set about drawing, like William (son of James) Playfair's statement that 'Nothing good in Architecture can be effected

without a monstrous effort of patience and India Rubber', are particularly revealing. Charles Cockerell wrote in his diary in 1824: 'The execution of these [plans for Mr Farquharson at Langton in Dorset] gave me great pleasure passing two days in the work. tho' to design is an effort & source of anxiety & fear the fruit is my chief pleasure — why should I affect to do any other kind of business.'[61] The picture of Charles Barry's working practice given by Alfred Barry and M.D. Wyatt is a valuable one. Barry seldom rose later than 6 a.m., and the hours until breakfast and from 8 a.m. until at the earliest 11 or 12 a.m. were always devoted the the drawing board. During the preparation of the Westminster competition drawings in 1835 he hardly had four or five hours' sleep in twenty-four. His first drawing for a scheme often contained all the essential details of the finished design. It would immediately be brought to the test of accurate scale drawing and enlarged details. The task of modification and alteration would then begin, generally tending after much labour to realise more fully and perfectly the concept of the first draft.

'Where we have an opportunity of tracing the progress of his thoughts through a series of studies for any particular building, we find the work growing, as it were, evenly under his hand from the slightest generalization in the first small-scale sketch, to the plotted-out bay or repeat, and subsequently to the large-scale detail: then back again to another general elevation, to see how far that particular detail will work well in combination, then altered according to the result of that test, and roughed out again on a large scale to make sure of the effect of the parts when near the eye, and so on, till his fastidious judgement would be almost bewildered under the multiplying and conflicting impressions produced by the various studies.'

Barry's weakness lay in his inability to delegate, and anything he did delegate he was soon impatient to see finished so that what he expected done in 'a couple of hours' became a proverb in the office.[62]

DRAUGHTSMANSHIP

'Working drawings', wrote Peter Nicholson in his

An Architectural Dictionary 'consist of plans, elevations, and sections, of the whole, and all the parts, of an edifice, to as large a scale as may be found convenient; generally in outline, except in the sectional parts, which are frequently shadowed, or scratched, in order to make them more obvious to the workman, for whose use the drawings are made.'[63]

Regency drawings survive in far greater quantities than do drawings from earlier in the eighteenth century. This is not chance but the result of a new attitude to the use of drawings which had its origins in the decades before 1790 when the establishment of English paper mills meant paper no longer had to be imported and so was cheaper and available in different sizes and qualities. When Burn was described as following Smirke's example in drawing out 'the plans with the minutest accuracy, dimensioning with his own hand every part and detail with peculiar clearness' he was following not only Smirke but Dance, Soane, Wyatville, Papworth and indeed any Regency architect whose drawings survive in quantity.

Through the use of detailed drawing Regency architects exercised a very direct control over their buildings. Like Burn their aim was 'to afford no excuse to the builder for any mistakes and blunders'. The volume of fifty-six contract drawings by Francis Edwards for St John the Baptist, Hoxton, of 1824 (85-96) contrasts strikingly with the relatively limited number provided by eighteenth-century ecclesiastical architects.

Regency architects also seem to have used far greater quantities of paper when designing. Cockerell's buildings can be traced through innumerable sketches of varying degrees of elaboration before a final design was reached (50-1), and the same was true of many of his contemporaries. Again, the origins of this can be found in the preceding decades. Cockerell records that James Wyatt 'Would make any no: of drawgs & destroy them for others with pleasure.'[64]

But quantity is not the only thing that distinguishes Regency drawings. 'In addition to the drawings, which are used in conducting the work, a perspective representation of the exterior should be furnished by the architect, in order to shew the general appearance and effect of the intended edifice to the employer.'[65] For Nicholson in 1819 the perspective was a standard tool of the architect, but its introduction was a radical innovation in British architectural draughtsmanship, a product not only of changing technique but of a new aesthetic sensibility.

When Thomas Sandby revealed one of his drawings of a Bridge of Magnificence to his audience as Professor of Architecture at the Royal Academy and stated that the 'perspective view is much more Picturesque than a Geometrical Elevation, and will shew its parts to better advantage' he was ushering in a revolution.[66] Drawings produced by neo-Palladian architects during the eighteenth century were uniformly executed in plan, elevation and section, as if they were taken from the pages of Palladio's *Four Books of Architecture*. The introduction of the perspective coincided with the end of that orthodoxy, and its replacement as the governing aesthetic by the Picturesque.

In 1807 Farington reported Benjamin West's statement that the style of drawing practised in England had been seen in no other country and that Sandby had originated it.[67] The style was the architectural perspective. Despite Chambers's experimentation with perspective drawings in Rome in the 1750s, he never used them in his practice, although he occasionally placed straight elevations in a landscape setting. Robert Adam did occasionally use perspectives, as in his design for Barnbougle of 1774 in the Earl of Rosebery's collection, but they were unusual.

Thomas Sandby never achieved their success, but as we have seen he was the first Professor of Architecture at the Royal Academy and also an accomplished topographical artist, used to making perspective drawings of buildings. And it was the grafting of this topographical tradition on to architectural design that created the architectural perspective.

In his first lecture Sandby declared that 'Perspective will, on many occasions, lend her assistance to the ingenious Artist, that he ought to obtain a competent knowledge thereof, as it represents & displays those happy forms in Buildings which produce an essential breath of light and shade; and at the same time enables the Artist to conceive, or know the true effect of his Designs in their various Situations and dispositions.' Sandby encouraged his students to get away from the Palladian obsession with the straight elevation and draw from life: 'Let me seriously recommend to the young Students in Architecture . . . that they accustom themselves to draw after real Buildings without the use of Rules and Compasses, in the manner of the Landskip Painters.' Whenever he mentioned architectural drawing Sandby stressed the desirability of a 'nearer approach to that of Nature.'[68]

It was in the 1790s that these ideas began to take hold. Thomas Malton's views of Sir Robert Taylor's buildings, both interiors and exteriors, must have created quite an impression at the Royal Academy in 1789-92. James Wyatt included a perspective, perhaps by Joseph Bonomi, in his designs for Henham Hall of 1793, now in the East Sussex Record Office. In 1794 John Nash submitted a perspective to the competition for Stafford County Hall. Soane recalled the impact that Sandby's teaching had on younger architects and was one of the first to produce perspectives of his work, doing so from the very beginning of his career in 1781. The first consistent practitioner was Joseph Bonomi who had served in Adam's office and may have been responsible for the perspectives in the first and second volumes of the *Works in Architecture of Robert and James Adam* of 1773 and 1779 that stand out so much from Adam's oeuvre.

Bonomi made his perspectives for the Royal Academy annual exhibition, his first appearance being in 1783. The importance of the annual exhibition in encouraging perspectives probably matched that of the Professor of Architecture, for architects were placed in direct comparison with the sort of paintings and drawings Sandby praised, and also in direct competition with each other. As Bonomi showed, the best way to make a drawing stand out was to make a picture of it (53). An inevitable result of competition was that architectural drawings grew larger as architects tried to give them greater impact.

But perspectives were not only drawn to entice clients, they had a role in design as well. Contemporary writers like Richard Brown, author of *The*

Principles of Practical Perspective (1815), stressed their importance in working out the effectiveness of a design, showing how a building would stand in a way that a straight elevation never could: 'a geometrical drawing alone without a perspective one is calculated to mislead, as the building will not appear to the eye when executed as it does on a geometrical elevation'.[69] As Sandby declared: 'it [perspective] seems the best method of sketching out the Idea for any Designs before a finished Drawing is made of such compositions'.[70]

Sandby's and Bonomi's drawings, like those of John Buckler (41), stand distinctly in the topographical tradition, clear and beautifully delineated, that dominated English watercolours in the 1770s and 80s. But the art of watercolour had moved beyond the clarity of Sandby before his death, for the years around the turn of the eighteenth century were years of rapid development, particularly as seen in the works of Cozens, Cotman, Girtin and Turner.

There were many links between the worlds of the watercolourist and the architectural draughtsman as Sandby had shown. Girtin and Turner both studied perspective under Thomas Malton, and Turner is believed to have added the background to some of Bonomi's works. John Varley taught watercolour to John Dobson and was asked by J.B. Papworth to add the background to his design for a 'Tropheum' to commemorate Waterloo. Papworth was the second secretary of the 'New Society of Painters in Miniature and Watercolour' founded in 1807, while A.C. Pugin was a member of the 'Old' Watercolour Society which had been founded in 1804. Papworth is an interesting case. According to James Thomson, who worked in his office, his drawings up to 1812 were in a style largely learnt from Chambers (who had lent him his drawings to copy as a boy) but his style then changed and was subsequently marked by its exquisite colouring and chiaroscuro.[71]

The greatest of the perspectivists was undoubtedly Joseph Gandy, whose architectural fantasies stood comparison with the work of any artist at the Royal Academy (2). But the bulk of Gandy's work was produced for Soane. From his first days Soane had realised that a successful architect would never have the time to produce good enough perspectives, a point which he made clear in his Royal Academy lectures: 'A superior manner of Drawing is absolutely necessary, indeed it is impossible not to admire the beauties and almost magical effects, in the architectural drawings of a Clerisseau, a Gandy, or a Turner. Few Architects, however, can hope to reach the excellency of those artists without devoting to Drawing too much of that time, which they ought to employ in the attainment of the higher and more essential qualifications of an Architect.'[72]

The result was an independent profession of architectural perspectivists, one of the earliest being A.C. Pugin who fled to England during the French Revolution. He answered an advertisement by Nash for a draughtsman around 1793: 'Perceiving that Pugin had taste and skill in the use of colours, he employed him on perspective views of buildings . . . These designs Pugin executed on a large scale in body colour, in a bold and effective manner.' Pugin's work was admired for its truthfulness of form and colour. As Benjamin Ferrey recorded:

'At this period there was a marked improvement perceptible in the work of artists who had previously worked in watercolours. The earlier practice in the art had been carried out with remarkable simplicity; broad tints of monotone, possessing something resembling a local tint, formed the groundwork, the objects being drawn freely with a reed pen, either in dark brown colour or Indian ink. So far this mode of working in watercolour had hitherto prevailed, but a change in the process now took place; the old method of preparing the drawing in uniform tint was given up, and efforts were made to represent objects with their local colours and varied effects of light and shade.'[73]

By the 1830s it was common for practices to employ perspectivists. Dobson used J.W. Carmichael, Salvin, James Deason; while in Rickman's office it was his partner Henry Hutchinson who made the perspectives.[74]

Perspectives were not without their critics. As early as 1809 the surveyor James Spiller complained in a letter to Soane about 'the effect which the fascinating drawings of otherwise unformed and inexperienced young men produce upon persons who are about to build'; adding that his draughtsmanship had not progressed beyond 'a geometrical drawing in Indian ink, and landscape'.[75]

By 1834 there was a distinct movement against the perspective and this is visible in an article 'On Certain deceptive Practices adopted by some Authors of Architectural Designs for Villas' written by 'An Observer' in the first volume of *The Architectural Magazine*. 'Every painter knows that by lights and shadows, by introducing forms in the trees and ground to contrast with those of the building, and in short, by working for effect, the most indifferent building may be made, by a clever artist, to appear handsome in the eyes of those who cannot refer effects to their causes.' The case began to build up against the perspective and in 1838 a committee set up by the Institute of British Architects to look into competitions recommended that 'In order to assist the judgement by establishing an uniform comparison, the drawings presented for competition should always be to one scale, and limited to one style of finishing, as in indian ink, with no colour, unless for such a purpose as that of distinguishing different materials in sections. Perspective drawings, if correctly made, are certainly desirable to show the proper effect of designs; but they should be restricted to specified points of view.'[76] But for the moment the perspective ruled supreme.

The third major development in architectural draughtsmanship during the Regency was that of colour coding to distinguish different building materials. Again, the origins of this can be found in the preceding decades, when it was used by all the leading architects. Robert Mylne used a careful system of colour coding — yellow for timber, light grey for the walls, dark grey for the chimney stacks, the main trusses in dark brown, metal ties in gunmetal — at Wormleybury in 1766. A drawing signed by James Adam dated 1774 shows the walls in orange, the timbers in yellow. Robert Adam's plans for altering Blackadder show the existing work in black and new work in pink. James Wyatt's plans for Badger Hall, dated March 1779, show existing work in black, new work in pink, timber in yellow and iron in blue. Chambers's drawings for Somerset House make similar uses of colour. James Playfair's drawings in the Soane Museum for altering Dalkeith House dated April 1786 also use colour coding, as do George Dance's drawings.[77]

But if colour coding was well established before 1790, it was during the Regency that it was developed into a full code and spread from the main practices to all levels of the profession, although there were as yet no published standards. As befits a pupil of Dance's Soane used colour coding from the beginning of his career. The designs for Tendring Hall, Suffolk, of 1784 in the Victoria & Albert Museum show him using pink, brown, green, yellow, blue and grey washes. He passed his system on to those in his office.

The drawings for St John, Hoxton (1824) by Francis Edwards are a good example of colour coding (88-90), but by then colour coding was becoming increasingly standard. It was principally used for sections, but could also be used to distinguish new from old work on plans, as in Wyatville's drawings for Dinton (32-3) of 1813, where the old work is in black, the new in pink, timber partitions in yellow and the joinery in the bookcases and side table in yellow. At Dinton the drawing was a design, but G.S. Repton used a similar scheme in his record drawings for Kitley House, Devon (42), and Hopkinson's Bank, London (123), with black for existing work, grey for new work and yellow for joinery such as doors and bookcases. Edward Crocker's plan of the coronation kitchens of 1821 is a particularly detailed example of colour in plans (56).

Colour coding was used for a slightly different purpose in antiquarian draughtsmanship where William Capon was one of the first to use colour to distinguish the work of one period from another.

RECORD DRAWINGS

For the architect all drawings were a potential source of future information. Most of Papworth's drawings were inscribed 'this drawing to be returned to the office of Mr Papworth'. To some clients this attitude came as a surprise, reflecting more their ambivalent approach to the role of the

architect than interest in the drawings themselves. One client wrote in 1825 'You also add that the Plans are considered as to be returned to Mr Papworth at my convenience. This is also unexpected by me — for I had supposed that paying for the Plans made them my property — and that I might then adopt or reject them wholly or partially as I might find convenient.' The supervisory role of the architect was clearly a novelty to him: 'I had imagined that the Plans being furnished by you, the remainder of the work rested between the Builder and the Surveyor.'

Papworth was incensed when, having broken with James Morrison for whom he had been working at Basildon Park, Berkshire, the solicitors insisted that all drawings relating to it be handed over. As his son complained: 'Such drawings, it is well known, are not of the slightest use to the Client after the work is completed, but are of some value to the Architect who wishes to preserve some record of his designs and labours without having recourse to the expense of making copies; and over each drawing he may have given loving care and attention, inappreciable to the great majority of clients, who can only understand the work when executed.'[78] This was the only occasion in Papworth's practice that the client demanded to keep the drawings.

Papworth wanted his drawings back to avoid the expense of copying them. Soane, on the other hand, kept copies of his designs from the earliest days of his practice. Eighteen volumes of his record drawings survive. They differ from design drawings by usually being made to a smaller scale and often lacking measurements. They include unexecuted schemes and are generally of elevations, plans or sections but include some perspectives. While such copies may have been partly kept with an eye for publication — some of the drawings in his book of 'Precedents' appear in his *Plans, Elevations and Sections of Buildings Erected in the Counties of Norfolk, Suffolk* of 1788 — most were made for his own record. The record drawings were made by Soane's pupils, as they were in Wightwick's office where record drawings were made from the executed plans, elevations, sections and details. Wightwick considered this an important part of his pupils' training.[79]

The origin of this practice is unclear, but again it lies in the decades before the Regency. It may be that some of Adam's drawings should be seen as record drawings. Two record books by James Wyatt survive in the Victoria & Albert and Metropolitan Museums. Soane was probably following the example of his former master Henry Holland, for whom he had worked between 1772 and 1778, three of whose volumes of record drawings survive in the RIBA (55). It would be interesting to know if Taylor kept record drawings but unfortunately his drawings which 'were left highly finished, and arranged in perfect series' have disappeared, apart from a volume of drawings of monuments and another of chimney-pieces in the Ashmolean Museum.[80] However, John Nash made his pupils take record drawings of all work in hand (58 and 72), and he may have taken the practice from Taylor in whose office he worked.[81]

A number of volumes of record drawings survive in the RIBA, including those of G.S. Repton while in Nash's office, of Thomas Cundy junior made in his father's office (61) and of William Donthorn which includes a number of houses on which he had worked in Wyatville's office (77-9).

Soane also had a practice of making topographical drawings recording finished work, particularly interiors (4-5) for which he usually commissioned J.M. Gandy. These were often exhibited at the Royal Academy and were subsequently hung in the Picture Room, Breakfast Room, North Dining Room and Model Room at Lincoln's Inn Fields. Soane was not alone in this: Farington records how the dining room at East Cowes Castle was hung with drawings of houses by Nash.[82]

FEES

James Noble's *The Professional Practice of Architects* (1836) has much useful information on architects' fees, and quotes the terms which Joseph Bonomi published in 1794.[83] Bonomi's letter to F.F. Turville in which he set out possible charges for additions to Bosworth Hall, Leicestershire, in 1789 is even more informative:

'My terms are, my Journeys paid; two guineas per day, during my stay in the Country; and the plans, fronts, sections, parts at full size for the execution of the work, and estimate (which I do in London) are to be paid separately, the amount of them, being a plain and small mansion, will be about thirty or forty pounds. My bringing any plan with me will be, I think, unnecessary, because, if the old house is to remain, then the alterations and additions must be made corresponding to it; and if it is to be intirely a new one, then I must consult your conveniences, the number and sizes of Rooms, etc., in short, during my little stay there, I shall make sketches enough, till they meet your approbation, especially as you are versed in Architecture, which gives me a great deal of pleasure.'

He clarified the matter in a subsequent letter: 'The information which you received from Ld. Dormer and Mr Weston, concerning my terms, agrees perfectly well with mine; because all the Drawings, Estimates etc. I make, during my short stay in the Country, I do not charge anything for: if the business is of such a nature, that can not be entirely finished in the course of those few days, then all the different drawings etc., that I am obliged to have done in Town, are to be paid extra.'[84]

In evidence given to the Select Committee of the House of Commons in 1828 Nash, Wyatville, Soane, Smirke, Cockerell, Seward, Pilkington, Henry Harrison and Thomas Hardwick all agreed that five per cent of the cost of the work was the accepted architect's charge. The three architects attached to the Office of Works received three per cent. There was some debate, however, on whether this percentage included measuring, for which Wyatville expected to be paid separately.[85] His additional charges were set out in a letter to General Murray:

'In regard to the architectural part of the business, my method has always been to receive a commission upon the actual expenditure, or upon a previous estimate, or computation of the probable cost, independent of my journies, for which I have been paid (for twenty years past) 2/6d per mile, out and home, which includes all expences and for time in travelling, thus making no difference to my

Employers whether one or more days are occupied in a journey, and it is also my rule to charge a whole journey if I have an appointment in the neighbourhood that enables me to pay a visit to any work in hand.'[86]

In 1806 he had charged two shillings per mile and three guineas a day when at a house, while James Wyatt was charging 2s 6d per mile and five guineas a day.[87]

For minor jobs Nash had a fixed scale of charges: three guineas for cottages, seven guineas for a farmhouse, fifteen guineas for a farmhouse and farmyard and ten guineas for lodges.[88]

SUCCESS

For the successful, architecture was a lucrative profession, and one with an increasingly high status. In 1828 Wyatville was the first architect since Wren to be knighted for his architectural achievement (Chambers was a knight of the Swedish order of the Polar Star, Taylor was given the customary knighthood for serving as Sheriff of London). Smirke and Soane followed in 1832. Joseph Bonomi told Farington in 1797 that he had saved £4,000 since setting up his practice in 1784.[89] George Dance's average income from his city surveyorship was £1,500 a year.[90] Wightwick averaged £1,000 a year as a provincial architect and in one year made £1,800.[91] Michael Searles's total income in 1792 must have been about £2,000.[92] John Sanders made enough to retire early and travel. Wyatville left £70,000, Smirke £90,000, and at the height of his career he was rumoured to be refusing commisions worth less than £10,000. The sums earned by Smirke are not surprising. At the Custom House, Post Office and British Museum alone he was handling commissions worth over £700,000 — on which his commission would work out at more than £21,000 — and the work laying out the approaches to the new London Bridge in 1829-35 must have been worth even more. Soane could afford to buy himself a villa at Pitzhanger, Ealing, London in 1801, and Nash reckoned that he was worth £100,000 in 1821.[93]

Nash was the prince of Regency architects. His first London house in Dover Street was noticeably wider than most terraced houses in Mayfair, his second house in Lower Regent Street was on the scale of a nobleman's *hôtel*. Between him and his relation Mr Edwards who shared it they had spent £34,000 on its construction. Farington noted with a certain awe that:

'in 33 years he had been able to purchase a farm in the Isle of Wight which he valued at 30,000; — East Cowes Castle & the land attached to it, he reckoned to be worth £30,000 — and that he has an extra £7,000 pr annm — He said [he had] 1100 shares in the *Regents Canal*. The shares are reckoned at £100 a share ... I measured the Vista in East Cowes Castle from the end of the dining room to the end of the Conservatory by stepping it and reckoned it to be 120 feet. — The Dining room is 30 feet by 20 and 15 feet high. I also measured the Terrace and found it 227 steps.'[94]

However, the last years of Nash's life were spent in a financial crisis.

PROFESSIONALISM

The financial success of a well-established profession went hand in hand with its professionalisation. That the newly formed Institute of British Architects should have received its royal charter in 1837, the year of Soane's death, was a fit conclusion to the Regency architectural profession. There had been various abortive attempts at such a body before, such as the Architects' Club of 1791, the London Architectural Society of 1806 and the Architects' and Antiquaries' Club of 1819, but none was a professional body aiming to represent all architects.

All his life Soane had fought for the professional standards of architects, and it was appropriate that he should have been offered the presidency of the new institute. Like Taylor before him Soane had consistently held to his belief that an architect should design and supervise the erection of a building but not involve himself in the contracting. Taylor was exceptional in his day for not contracting; Chambers, Adam and Paine all did. So did some of the leading Regency figures. Wyatville followed the example of his uncles James and Samuel Wyatt and was a contractor as well as architect. Nash certainly saw no reason why the same man should not be architect, speculator and builder and supplier, and created considerable controversy when a firm of brickmakers with which he was involved supplied the works at Buckingham Palace. But Soane's example prevailed. The new generation of architects such as Smirke and Charles Cockerell were solely architects and anyone engaged in contracting or profiting from it was disbarred from the new Institute.

NOTES

THE key source for the study of Regency architects is Howard Colvin's *Biographical Dictionary of British Architects* (1978). As this is arranged with an entry for each architect footnotes have not been made for references which can be found there.

1 RIBA Ms WiG/1/2 George Wightwick, *The Life of an Architect*, 148.
2 Guildhall Library, Index to the Apprenticeship Records in the Public Record Office.
3 RIBA Ms Coc 9/3 f. 11.
4 'An Essay on the Qualifications and Duties of an Architect', quoted in B. Kaye, *The Development of the Architectural Profession in Britain*, London, 1960, 48-50.
5 B. Ferrey, *Recollections of A.N. Welby Pugin, and his father Augustus Pugin; with notices of their works*, London, 1861, 26-9.
6 G.G. Scott, *Personal and Professional Recollections*, London, 1879, 55-6.
7 A.T. Bolton, *Architectural Education a Century Ago*, London, n.d., 3.
8 J. Soane, *Lectures on Architecture*, ed. A.T. Bolton, London, 1929, 103.
9 RIBA Ms WiG/1/2 George Wightwick, *The Life of an Architect*, 23, 34-6.
10 RIBA Coc 9/5, 25 February.
11 T.L. Donaldson, 'Memoir of the late William Burn' in *Transactions of the Royal Institute of British Architects*, 1869-70, 121-9.
12 Scott, 73.
13 L. Aikin, *Memoir of John Aikin*, I, London, 1823, 267-72.
14 Scott, 56-7.
15 W. Papworth, *John B. Papworth*, London, 1879, 7.
16 RIBA Ms WiG/1/2 George Wightwick, *The Life of an Architect*, 35; A. Barry, *The Life and Works of Sir Charles Barry*, London, 1867, 6; Scott, 48.
17 Scott, 66.
18 RIBA Ms Coc 9/5 f. 72.
19 Soane, 15.
20 Scott, 58.
21 G.L. Taylor, *The Auto-biography of an Octogenarian Architect*, London, 1870, 1.
22 A. Graves, *The Royal Academy of Arts*, I, London, 1905, 130.
23 Soane, 91.
24 T.L. Donaldson, *A Review of the Professional Life of Sir John Soane*, London, 1837, 20.

25 Scott, 66.
26 Scott, 71-3.
27 Gandy Green Book, p. 17, quoted in *Joseph Michael Gandy (1771-1843)*, Catalogue of an Exhibition at the Architectural Association, 1982, 26.
28 RIBA Ms WiG/1/2 George Wightwick, *The Life of an Architect*, 71-85.
29 K. Cave (ed.), *The Diary of Joseph Farington*, XIII, 1984, 4728.
30 Scott, 71.
31 M. Dobson, *Memoir of John Dobson*, London, 1885, 15.
32 A.T. Bolton, *The Portrait of Sir John Soane*, London, 1927, 229.
33 Taylor, iv.
34 RIBA Ms Coc 9/5 ff. 53-4.
35 Scott, 73.
36 C. Proudfoot and D. Watkin, 'A Pioneer of English neo-Classicism', *Country Life*, 13/20 April 1972.
37 N. Temple, *John Nash and the Village Picturesque*, Gloucester, 1979, 132-7.
38 RIBA Ms WiG/1/2, 113-14, 158.
39 Barry, 64.
40 Papworth, 118.
41 Papworth, 122.
42 James Noble, *The Professional Practice of Architects*, London, 1836, 33-5.
43 Papworth, 99.
44 Bolton, 1927, 57.
45 Scott, 78-9.
46 J.M. Crook, 'Architect of the Rectangular', *Country Life*, 4 April, 1967.
47 Dobson, 15, 35.
48 Farington, III, 841; Farington, XVI, 5744; Horace Walpole, *Anecdotes of Painting*, ed. Hilles and Daghlian, V, London, 1937, 195.
49 Farington, XVI, 5746.
50 Scott, 78-9; Dobson, 16-17; Barry, 324; Papworth, 99.
51 M. Richardson, 'Soane's Use of Drawings', *Apollo*, April, 1990.
52 W. Bonwitt, *Michael Searles, A Georgian Architect and Surveyor*, London, 1987, 28.
53 J.M. Robinson, *The Wyatts, An Architectural Dynasty*, Oxford, 1979, 70; *Catalogue of the Drawings Collection of the RIBA C-F*, Farnborough, 1972, 59; Farington, XII, 4246; Richardson, 'Soane's Use of Drawings'; D. Watkin, *The Life and Work of C.R. Cockerell*, London, 1974, 42.
54 Bolton, *Architectural Education a Century Ago*, London,

n.d., 12-19; Bolton, 1927, 51.

55 Watkin, 42.

56 Farington, XV, 5134.

57 Dobson, 14-15.

58 Richardson, 'Soane's Use of Drawings'.

59 D. Linstrum, *Sir Jeffry Wyatville*, Oxford, 1972, 24-6.

60 Donaldson, 1869-70, 121-9.

61 RIBA Ms Coc 9/5 f. 44.

62 Barry, 86, 326.

63 Peter Nicholson, *An Architectural Dictionary*, II, London, 1819, 808.

64 J. Harris, 'C.R. Cockerell's "Ichnographica Domestica"' in *Architectural History*, XIV, 1971, 14.

65 Nicholson, I, 412.

66 RIBA Ms SaT/1/1 'Six Lectures by Thomas Sandby read at the Royal Academy 1794', Lecture Six f. 48.

67 Farington, VIII, 2998.

68 RIBA Ms SaT/1/1 First Lecture f. 38.

69 R. Brown, *The Principles of Practical Perspective*, London, 1815, ix.

70 RIBA Ms SaT/1/1 First Lecture f. 38.

71 Papworth, 17, 28-30.

72 Bolton, 1927, 88.

73 Ferrey, 2, 6-7.

74 T. Faulkener and A. Greg, *John Dobson, Newcastle Architect, 1787-1865*, Newcastle, 1987, 95; J. Allibone, *Anthony Salvin, Pioneer of Gothic Revival Architecture, 1799-1881*, Columbia, 1987, 19; RIBA Ms Rickman diaries 4 February, 1830.

75 Bolton, 1927, 103.

76 Quoted by G. Stamp, *The Great Perspectivists*, London, 1982, 15.

77 RIBA Drawings Collection RAN/1/J/2, K12/1, K12/7, J4/6; Soane Museum, Slider IV.2/6, IV.3/4, IV.4/9/5.

78 Papworth, 91-2, 102.

79 RIBA Ms WiG/1/2 f. 173.

80 M. Binney, *Sir Robert Taylor*, London, 1984, 16.

81 RIBA Ms Coc 9/5 f. 53-4.

82 Farington, XVI, 5746.

83 Noble, 174-5.

84 Peter Meadows, *Joseph Bonomi, Architect, 1739-1808*, London, 1988, 12.

85 Noble, 32-5.

86 Linstrum, 27.

87 Farington, VIII, 2887.

88 J. Summerson, *The Life and Work of John Nash*, Cambridge, 1980, 51.

89 Farington, III, 881.

90 *Catalogue of the Drawings Collection of the RIBA C-F*, Farnborough, 1972, 59.

91 RIBA Ms WiG/1/2 f. 158.

92 Bonwitt, 28.

93 Farington, XVI, 5745.

94 Farington, XVI, 5745-6.

ARCHITECTURAL
DRAWINGS OF THE
REGENCY PERIOD

1790–1837

I   PUBLIC BUILDINGS

For most of the eighteenth century major public building had eluded architects. The Palace of Whitehall was never rebuilt, nor were the Houses of Parliament. The Horse-guards were replaced but Kent's Treasury was left half-finished. Somerset House, begun in 1776, heralded a change. Here was a governmental building on a scale comparable with anything on the Continent. The outbreak of war with France in 1793 forced the government to redirect its efforts and vast sums were poured into building barracks, forts and naval dockyards. More than £4 million were spent on barracks alone between 1792 and 1804.

With military expenditure on such a scale, civic architecture had to be put aside, except where it was relevant to the war effort. As the national debt soared to pay for the war the Bank of England went from strength to strength, and a great series of banking halls were added by John Soane to service the new demand for bank stock (5). The Royal Mint was reformed and rebuilt on a fresh site between 1806 and 1811 at a final cost of nearly £300,000 (9-11). These were years when British possessions in India were increasing swiftly, and to ensure their effective governance East India House, headquarters of the East India Company, was rebuilt from 1796.

Other projects like James Lewis's plans for rebuilding Christ's Hospital in 1795 (21) were frustrated by war, but the economy continued to grow

strongly. There was enough money to rebuild both Covent Garden Theatre after it was burnt down in 1808 and the Theatre Royal, Drury Lane after that was burnt down in 1809 (24-6). But this had nothing on the wave of expenditure that surged in the decades that followed peace. James Thomson, who joined J.B. Papworth's office in 1812 recalled the change from the perspective of old age:

'The long war with France had come to its triumphant close, and the vast capital required for so many years and spent in arms, ammunition, and on men, was gradually withdrawn, to be devoted to peaceful purposes. This to a country like England, mistress of the commerce of the world, soon began to tell in the buildings, both public and private, of the metropolis, and not only them but in most of the commercial cities of the empire: so that London, taking the City and Westminster, had nearly every great public edifice built or rebuilt.'

Foreigners were amazed that a country that had been at war for so long could afford to spend so much on public architecture, and the decades after Waterloo were years of unparalleled public patronage. The 1820s were without precedent in British architecture. A new palace was built in 1825-30 at a cost of over £600,000. Over £1 million was spent on Windsor Castle between 1824 and 1840. Smirke's General Post Office begun in 1824 cost £200,000.

In 1823 he had begun the British Museum on the most massive scale. Soane effectively rehoused all three elements of the government — legislative, executive and judiciary — with a new royal entrance, royal gallery, library and committee rooms for the House of Lords in 1822-7; new library and committee rooms for the House of Commons in 1826-7; new Board of Trade and Privy Council offices in 1824-6; and new law courts in 1822-5 (4). An entire new university, University College, London, was begun to the designs of William Wilkins in 1827. Outside London, £30,000 was spent on a new custom house and excise office at Greenock in 1817-18 (7-8). All this was capped by the rebuilding of the Palace of Westminster following its destruction by fire in 1834, but as that story lies mainly in the reign of Queen Victoria it has been left to the next volume of this series.

The government was not alone in spending on this scale. The Fish-mongers' Company, whose hall was demolished for the rebuilding of London Bridge, set aside £50,000 to build a new hall (30). And £43,000 was spent on building just one club, the Athenaeum (27-9). This was typical of the way private architecture was taking on the scale of public buildings. Education and the arts profited from a rash of new building. In virtually every city a body such as the Bristol Philosophical and Literary Institution (31) was founded or given new quarters so that citizens could keep abreast of the latest advances in the arts and sciences. Some were part museums like the Manchester Institution, but these decades also saw the erection of several of our greatest public galleries, not only the British Museum but the National Gallery in 1834, and the Fitzwilliam Museum in Cambridge in the same year (15-17).

Incipient reform in public schools led to Barry's rebuilding of King Edward VI's School, Birmingham, spurred on by an ambitious headmaster in 1833 (23). In Bedford Blore had already begun rebuilding the English School for the Harpur Trust (22).

Hospitals were one of the few types of major building that had been built in relatively large numbers in the eighteenth century, but the campaigns of John Howard showed these up as inadequate, and the Regency saw the first of the great series of hospitals and lunatic asylums that are such a mark of nineteenth-century public health care (12-14). Workhouses were set up to cope with the uncomfortable increase in the number of paupers that accompanied rapid industrialisation (20).

Such an outbreak of public and semi-public building was not without controversy. The vast sums spent on the royal palaces, particularly on Buckingham Palace, were severely criticised in Parliament. Soane was forced to alter his design for the new law courts after work had begun because of attacks in Parliament and the press. Style was increasingly controversial, with the Greek Revival first coming to prominence with two highly publicised buildings, Downing College and Smirke's Covent Garden Theatre, although Thomas Harrison's work at Chester predates both. The Greek Revival, with its austere air of grandeur seemed an appropriate style for public buildings, as Burn showed at the Custom House and Excise Office at Greenock (7-8). It only lasted a couple of decades, but the classical tradition was still strong at the end of the Regency. Goldicutt's competition design for the Fishmongers' Hall (30) shows its vitality, as does Basevi's Fitzwilliam Museum. Some of the best classical work, particularly that of Cockerell was still to come, but by 1837 the future lay with Barry and Pugin's Gothic at King Edward's School (23) and with Burn's Jacobean at the Royal Crichton Institute (12-14).

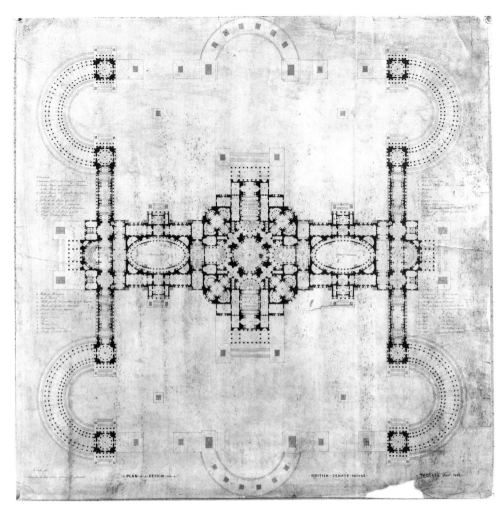

Thomas Lee 1794-1834
Design for a British senate house
1 Plan, 1816
Pen and coloured washes
(620 × 630)

THIS design, for which a section
and elevation also survive in the
Drawings Collection, won Lee the
gold medal at the Society of Arts in
1816. The drawing would have been
submitted anonymously, with the
motto *'Forsam, et haec olim meminisse
juvabit'* to identify the draughtsman.
Name, date and description must
have been added later.

Ideal designs for buildings on this
scale, in particular senate houses,
palaces or triumphal bridges, were a
popular subject for architectural competitions. This was a longstanding
Continental tradition that was
brought to England in the late eighteenth century, first at the Society of
Arts and then at the Royal Academy,
to help stimulate a more professional
approach to the training of young
architects. Success would bring them
to public attention at a time when
they were training or working in
another architect's office or were
trying to establish an independent
practice. In the same year Lee also
won the Royal Academy's silver
medal for a drawing of Chiswick
House, and in 1820 he tried to win
the Academy's gold medal with a
reconstruction of Pliny's villa at
Laurentinum.

Lee's father, also Thomas, had
trained as an architect, winning the
Royal Academy's silver medal in
1776. He had never practised because
he had come into money as a young
man, but his son was trained under
Soane and then under David Laing, a
former pupil of Soane's. He was
admitted to the Royal Academy
schools in 1812. Although Lee was
only briefly in Soane's office his design was heavily indebted to that
Soane submitted to the Royal
Academy in 1779 for a British
senate house.

Lee subsequently established his
own practice based principally in his
native West Country and in the
West Midlands, but drowned bath-
ing in 1834.

Joseph Michael Gandy 1771-1843
Design for an imperial palace for
sovereigns of the British Empire
2 Perspective, 1824-8
Watercolour (760 × 1345)

LIKE Lee's senate designs, this is
an ideal scheme produced for exhibition, this time at the Royal Academy.
But whereas Lee's was a competition
drawing done by a young man at the
start of his career, by 1824 Gandy
was fifty-three.

Gandy's career had started auspi-
ciously. His skill as a draughtsman
and his remarkable architectural imagination had won him the silver
medal at the Royal Academy schools
in 1789 and the gold medal the
following year. Sent out to Rome in
the company of C.H. Tatham he had
won a special medal at the Academy
of St Luke. But his attempt to establish an independent practice was not
a success. Instead he earned his keep
making perspectives for Soane and
engaged his imagination in
architectural fantasies. He exhibited
an almost unbroken series of these at
the Royal Academy between 1789
and 1838. Four palace designs were
shown between 1824 and 1827.

The idea of a royal palace must
have been in the air. The new king,
George IV, had been considering
employing John Nash to rebuild
Buckingham House since 1821, and
work began in 1825. Soane, who had
already designed two ideal palaces
and who considered it his right as
architect in charge of Buckingham
House to build the new palace, had
made his own designs in 1821.

Although it is assumed that these
are fantasies, Gandy provided an
estimate which suggests that he considered them practical if, at £3
million, improbable. Even Nash's
notoriously expensive works at Buckingham Palace only cost £613,269.

Thomas Harrison 1744-1829
Design for a monumental gateway
3 Elevation, n.d.
Pen with sepia and yellow washes
(415 × 650)

A<small>LTHOUGH</small> he never practised in London, Harrison was the first English architect to grasp the full potential of the Greek Revival. Marrying this with contemporary French ideas he created some of the finest neoclassical architecture of the Regency. His most important work was at Chester Castle where between 1788 and 1822 he created a complex of county courts, armoury, barracks, exchequer and gateway that have no rival during the period.

C.R. Cockerell, the finest classical architect of his day, considered that Harrison had 'a spark divine', and his first biographer Canon Blomfield was accurate when he wrote that Harrison was 'Almost, if not quite, the first architectural genius in the Kingdom.'

Harrison's career differs from that of his contemporaries for he does not seem to have been apprenticed as an architect, but was sent to Rome in 1769 thanks to the patronage of a local landowner, Sir Lawrence Dundas. His years there were formative, and he returned in 1776 a master of the contemporary continental neoclassical style. His achievement was to marry this with a thorough, but unpedantic, understanding of Greek architecture. After practising first in Lancaster he settled in Chester in 1793. His work is concentrated in the North-West, and a natural diffidence prevented wider acclaim.

This design is uninscribed but may relate to designs for George III's jubilee memorial project of 1810 now in Chester Public Library.

View of the Entrance to the Court of Exchequer

Sir John Soane 1753-1837
Topographical view of the Court of
the Exchequer, Westminster,
London
4 Interior perspective by
C.J. Richardson 1809-1872, 1825
Pencil and pen (315 × 245)

Soane was appointed one of the three 'Attached Architects' to the board of works in 1814 with particular responsibility, among other buildings, for Westminster. Thus he was the architect of the new law courts erected in 1822-5 and demolished in 1883. The site was small and constricted by Westminster Hall and other existing buildings, but Soane's skilful planning made space for the seven chief law courts, five placed between the great buttresses of Westminster Hall, all masterly variations on the theme of the toplit room.

Soane always had topographical drawings made of his buildings after they were finished. We know from the office daybooks that C.J. Richardson spent much of October and November 1825 'making sketches of the New Courts at Westminster', which must have included this drawing. A watercolour based on it is in the Soane Museum, dated 12 August 1826. This and the other preparatory sketches are bound into a privately printed copy of Soane's *Civil Architecture, Designs for Completing Some of the Public Buildings in Westminster and for Correcting Defects in Others* which was presented to the RIBA by S. Vacher from the library of his father, the stationer Thomas Vacher. Although the book is inscribed 'From the Author 4th May 1829' Vacher is not on the list of those to whom Soane presented a copy, and so he must have bought it later, presumably then binding in the sketches of the law courts. These had probably been kept by Richardson who began to sell drawings from the Soane office in the 1860s, most of his collection ending up in the Victoria & Albert Museum.

Sir John Soane 1753-1837
Topographical drawing of the
interior of the 3% Consols Office of
the Bank of England, City of London
5 Perspective by Henry Seward
c. 1778-1848, 1800
Watercolour (455 × 605)

THE rebuilding and extension of
the Bank of England by Soane between 1788 and 1833 reveals the
increasing financial importance of
the Bank and the City of London,
spurred on by governmental demands for borrowing to finance the
Napoleonic Wars. Four great halls to
handle the sale of stock were built in
the 1790s, with a further hall added
in 1818. All were essays in toplight-
ing and in Soane's idiosyncratic use
of domes and astylar decoration.
They were demolished between 1930
and 1940.

This drawing is inscribed *September 2 1800* and the Soane office
daybooks reveal that Henry Seward
spent three days from 30 August to *2
September 1800* 'About Perspective
View of Transfer Office'. A view of
the 3% Consols Office, presumably
by Gandy, was exhibited at the Royal
Academy in the spring of 1800 and
this drawing was probably a copy
made either as part of Seward's training or to be a gift from Soane. That
would explain why the drawing is
uncharacteristically signed *John Soane
Archt 1799*, the year that the 3%
Consols Office was completed.

In comparison with Gandy's superb draughtsmanship this drawing
is weakly executed, but it still catches
the drama of Soane's interior.

Attributed to William Wilkins
1778-1839
Design for a monument
to the Duke of York in The Mall,
Westminster, London
6 Perspective, *c.* 1827
Watercolour (450 × 645)

ALTHOUGH best known as the subject of the derogatory nursery rhyme, the Duke of York was an immensely popular commander-in-chief of the Army, and on his death in 1827 it was decided to erect a monument to him. There are various schemes in the RIBA Drawings Collection for a monument in Whitehall in front of the Horseguards, and Soane designed a tempietto with a statue of the Duke in St James's Park. Benjamin Wyatt considered a monument in the form of a Corinthian temple reusing the columns from Carlton House at the bottom of Lower Regent Street, and Wilkins's design follows the same idea. In the end Benjamin Wyatt built the existing column looking out over The Mall. This drawing was probably made by a professional perspectivist rather than Wilkins himself.

Wilkins had travelled extensively in Greece and Asia Minor, and with his triumph at Downing College in 1807, where his rigorously Greek designs were preferred to James Wyatt's more Roman scheme, established himself as a leader of the Greek Revival. Wilkins was seldom successful in turning his immense scholarship into successful architecture, and much of his work, such as the National Gallery or St George's Hospital, is disappointing. In this design he put aside the austerity of the Greek Doric for the more elegant Corinthian.

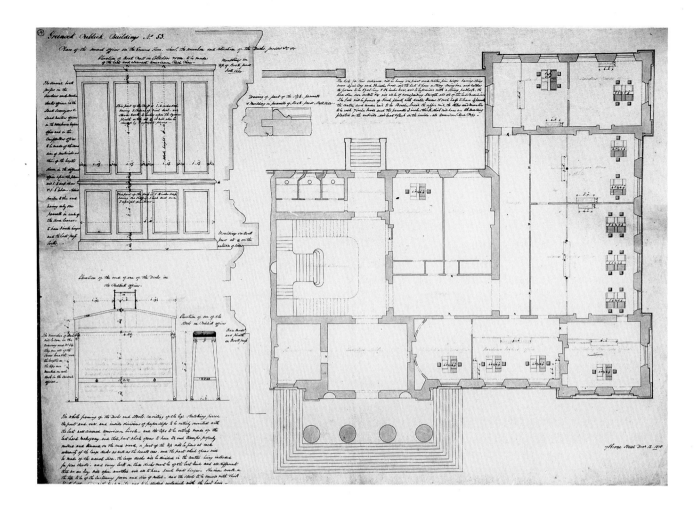

William Burn 1789-1870
Contract drawing for Greenock
Custom House and Excise Office,
Strathclyde
7 Plan of offices on ground floor with
details of the furniture, 1818
Pen, red pen and coloured washes
(515 × 720)

THE son of an Edinburgh architect and builder, William Burn was apprenticed in 1808 to Robert Smirke, then just beginning his career. On his return to Edinburgh in 1811 or 1812 Burn soon established himself as one of Scotland's leading architects. By 1840 he had already designed or altered over ninety country houses, thirty churches and twenty-five public buildings. The Greenock Custom House and Excise Office was his first major commission, and meant that he felt secure enough in his career to marry.

Burn's earliest works show the strong influence of Smirke, and the Custom House is particularly indebted to Smirke's Covent Garden Theatre on which Burn would have worked while in London. Its austerity and noble Doric portico seemed to symbolise public service. Indeed buildings of the Greek Revival were well suited for public works as their austerity meant that expensive architectural detail could be kept to a minimum. But even before 1837 taste had moved towards greater elaboration in public architecture, as was to be symbolised by Barry's Houses of Parliament, designed at the very end of the Regency period. Similarly, Burn's later work was to show great freedom of style, and he followed the complete spectrum of nineteenth-century stylistic development from the Greek Revival in the second decade of the century to the Scottish Baronial in the 1860s.

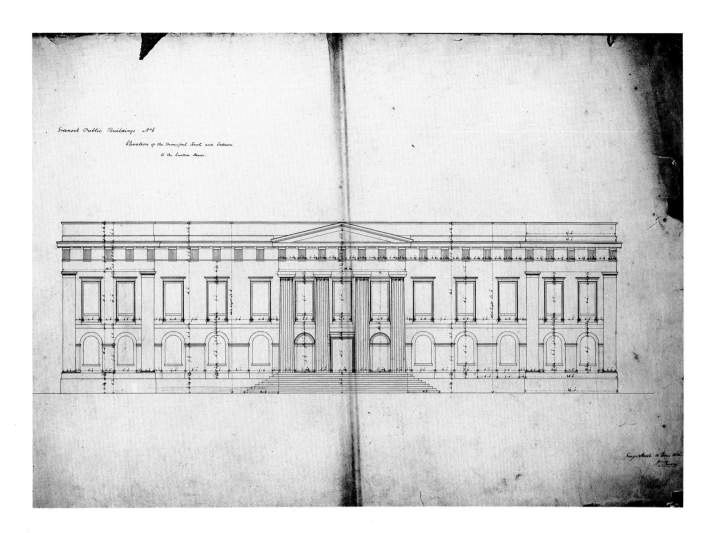

Greenock Public Buildings N° 6

Elevation of the Principal Front and Entrance
to the Custom House.

William Burn 1789-1870
Contract drawing for Greenock
Custom House and Excise Office,
Strathclyde
8 Principal elevation of the Custom
House, 1816
Pen (540 × 800)

GREENOCK suffered from the loss
of the North American colonies, but
soon recovered through increased
trade with South America and the
East and West Indies. A series of
new docks was built and the town
grew swiftly so that by 1841 it had

nearly forty thousand inhabitants.
The new Custom House and Excise
Office is proof of that prosperity.
However, even by then trade was
suffering from the deepening of the
Clyde and the introduction of steam
tugs which allowed ocean-going ves-
sels to penetrate as far as Glasgow.
The foundation stone of the Custom
House was laid with masonic hon-
ours on 2 May 1817, and the shell
finished the following year. The total
cost of the building was approximately £30,000.

The drawing is dated 10 June 1816,
and an inscription on its back declares
that this is plan number six as referred
to in the contract. The RIBA Drawings Collection has twenty-one of at

least fifty-four such drawings. They
were signed on 31 March 1817 by
each of the contractors to show they
were in agreement. Even the placing
of the desks and the design of the
furniture is carefully shown. This
attention to detail had been learnt
from Smirke as T.L. Donaldson's
memoir of Burn recalled: 'He sketched with great accuracy and neatness,
and following the example of his
master Sir Robert Smirke, he in his
earliest works at least drew out the
plans with the minutest accuracy,
dimensioning with his own hand every part and detail with peculiar
clearness, so as to afford no excuse to
the builder for any mistakes or blunders.'

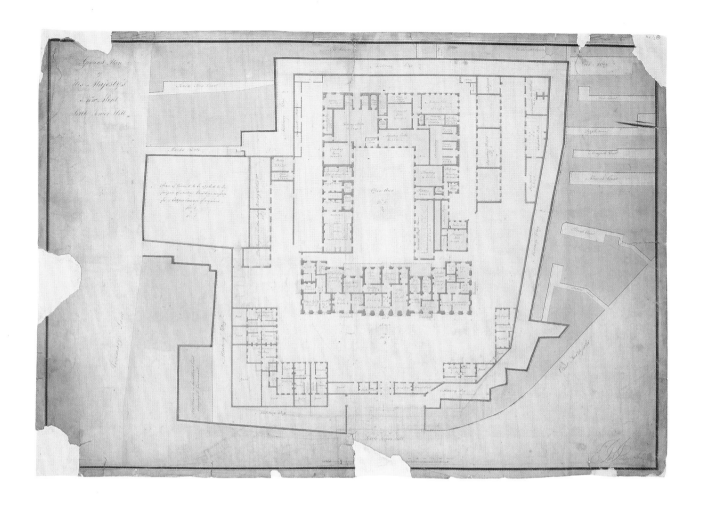

James Johnson ? -1807
Design for the Royal Mint, Tower
Hill, Tower Hamlets, London
9 Plan, 1806
Pen and coloured washes
(560 × 815)

10 Elevation of the rear facade, 1806
Pen and coloured washes
(610 × 1005)

11 Three transverse sections, 1806
Pen and coloured washes
(615 × 1035)

JOHNSON was appointed surveyor to the Mint in 1794. He was also architect to the barrack department of the War Office. The Mint was in serious need of reform, its buildings were crumbling, its machinery outdated and its working practices antiquated. The decision was taken to leave the confines of the Tower for a new site just to the north. Plans were drawn and the shell of the main block had been completed when Johnson died. He was replaced by Robert Smirke. Smirke modified the design, but the basic plan and main facade remained Johnson's. The plan (9) is pricked for copying, and the sections are interesting for their use of colour coding, pink for stone, dark brown for the foundations, light brown for timber, blue for slates and grey for plaster.

Work continued until 1811, with repeated parliamentary inquiries into the ever-increasing price. An original estimate of £126,490 proved hopelessly out, and the final figure was £288,656, not including the cost of buying and installing the machinery. The Mint was extended in 1881-2, and has recently been the centre of a commercial redevelopment which has kept the main block.

ELEVATION OF THE BACK FRONT OF HIS MAJESTY'S MINT LITTLE TOWER HILL

Scale of — feet

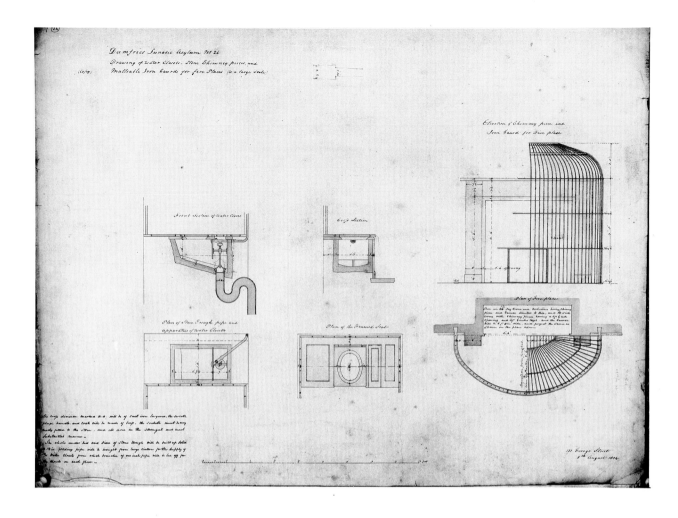

William Burn 1789-1870

Working drawings for the Crichton
Royal Institution, Dumfries, Dumfries and Galloway

12 Plans and sections of a water
closet and plan and elevation of a
chimney-piece and fireguard, 1834
Pen and coloured washes
(480 × 640)

13 Elevation of the east front, 1834
Pen and coloured washes
(640 × 975)

14 Plan of the principal floor, 1834
Pen, red pen and coloured washes
(625 × 965)

THE Crichton Royal Institution
was established by Mrs Elizabeth
Crichton from the £100,000 left her
by her husband. It was erected in
1834-9 and held the reputation of
being the best lunatic asylum in Scotland. Hospitals were among the
largest buildings erected during the
eighteenth century, but as the re-
marks of the prison reformer John
Howard, in his *Account of the Principal Lazarettos in Europe* of 1789,
show, size was no guarantee of effectiveness. The Crichton Royal Institution is typical of the enormous insti-
tutional buildings that Howard's
campaigns inspired in the nineteenth
century, in particular hospitals, lunatic asylums and prisons. Radial plans
were popular in all these types of
buildings.

These designs, which come mid-
way in Burn's career, make an interesting comparison with those for
the Greenock Custom House (7-8).
Both show the same attention to
detail and clear presentation of all
aspects of the design. The Custom
House, built at the height of the
Greek Revival, has a noble Greek
Doric portico, but by the 1830s public buildings were being designed in a
vaguely Jacobean style.

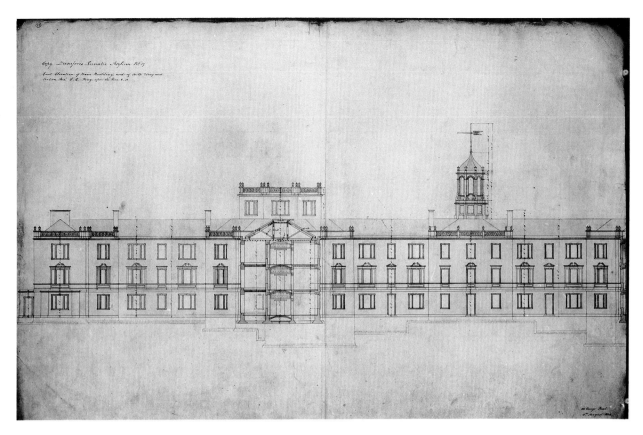

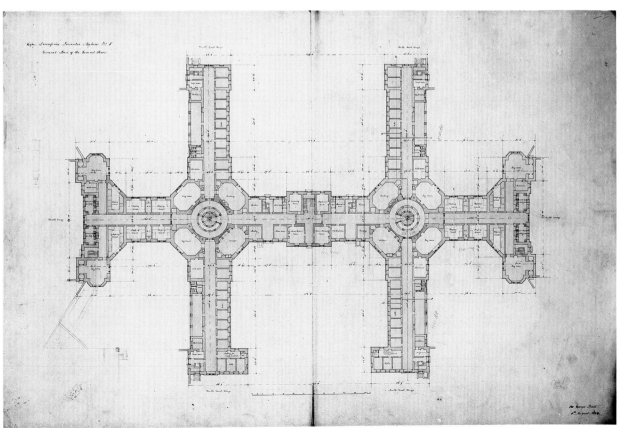

**Thomas Rickman 1776-1841 and
Richard Charles Hussey 1802-1887**
Competition designs for the
Fitzwilliam Museum, Cambridge
15 Design B. Perspective, 1835
Watercolour (745 × 520)

16 Design A. Perspective, 1835
Watercolour (300 × 525)

Henry Duesbury *fl.* **1832-1850**
Competition design for the
Fitzwilliam Museum, Cambridge
17 Perspective, 1835
Watercolour (475 × 930)

Twenty-seven architects submitted designs for the Fitzwilliam Museum competition which was won by George Basevi. Duesbury's design is closely based on Soane's Lothbury front of the Bank of England, but apart from this perspective he is almost unknown.

Rickman and Hussey were an extremely prolific practice based in Birmingham. The first reference to the competition in Rickman's timebooks comes on 2 August 1834, and eleven days later Rickman visited Cambridge to discuss the project with the Vice-Chancellor.

He set to work at once, examining plans and an elevation, presumably sketches, on 20 August, but the bulk of the work was done in February and the first half of March when virtually every day included work done on the Fitzwilliam. All was finished by 17 March, and on 7 April Rickman set off for Cambridge. On the ninth he examined the drawings for the last time, signed the report and packed them up, delivering them to the Vice-Chancellor the following day. Despite putting forward three different schemes in Gothic, Roman Doric and Grecian styles, with a selection of interiors, his designs did not meet favour. The Grecian scheme received forty-four votes, the Gothic one only three. Basevi's winning design had 140 votes.

It is uncertain who Rickman used to make these perspectives, which are clearly in different hands.

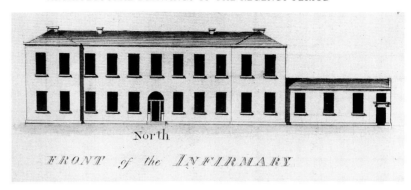

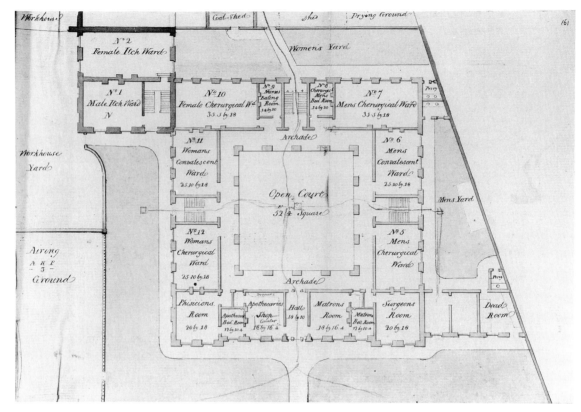

John White c. 1747-1813
Record drawings of St Marylebone
Infirmary, Northumberland Street,
Westminster, London
18 Elevation of the north front,
c. 1793
Pen and coloured washes
(150 × 190)

19 Groundfloor plan, *c.* 1793
Pen and coloured washes
(185 × 280)

WHITE was less an architect than a surveyor and developer. As surveyor to the Duke of Portland he laid out the Portland estate in Marylebone from 1787, while at the same time acting as one of the principal contractors. It was as surveyor that he designed first the Marylebone Parish Workhouse in 1775 and then added this infirmary to it in 1793-4. White had a particular interest in the welfare of the poor in the parish and gave his design for the infirmary free.

White's drawings, as befit a sur-veyor, are simple and practical. They come from a small record volume containing plans and elevations of various buildings by White, some of them with details of costs. The total cost of the Infirmary came to £6,788 6s 5¼d, of which Roberts and Ban-ner received £2,688 for bricklaying, and a further £1,074 for masonry, and John Spink £1,781 for carpentry. The plastering was done by John Papworth, father of John Buonarotti Papworth. Both workhouse and infir-mary were demolished in the 1890s.

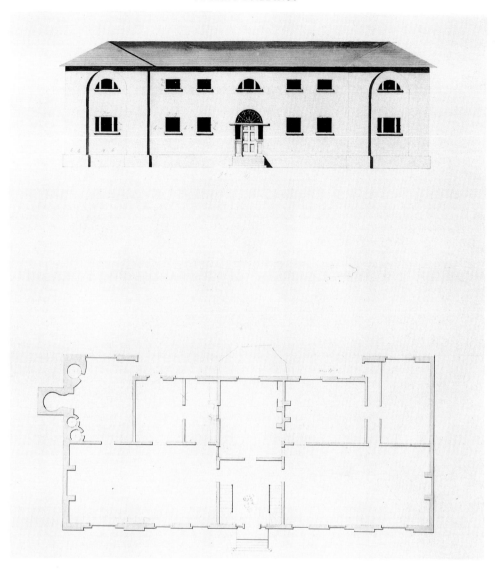

Michael Searles 1750-1813
Design for Streatham Workhouse,
Lambeth, London
20 Plan and principal elevation, 1790
Pen and coloured washes with pencil
additions (625 × 505)

Searles obtained the commission to design a workhouse for the Parish of Streatham through two of the parish's Overseers or Guardians of the Poor for whom he had already worked. These initial designs were not accepted, but the executed scheme, now in the Lambeth Archives, differs only in details. Unfortunately, Searles failed to supervise the construction with sufficient care and the whole matter ended up at the Guildford Assizes.

Although the Streatham Guardians had to obtain a special Act of Parliament to erect the workhouse, workhouses became increasingly common as the government and the localities struggled to cope with the pauperisation that accompanied the agricultural and industrial revolutions. Between 1784 and 1818 the payment of poor rates increased three times as fast as the population. Workhouses were seen as a way to control the problem and their establishment in every part of the country was the centre of the Poor Law Act of 1834.

Searles was the son of a surveyor and followed in his father's profession, establishing himself in Bermondsey where he was surveyor to the Rolls estate. A large collection of his drawings survive in the RIBA, illuminating that area of the architectural profession which is least documented, that of the minor metropolitan surveyor-architect.

James Lewis *c.* **1751-1820**
Design for Christ's Hospital,
City of London
21 Principal elevation, *c.* 1795
Pen and watercolour
(390 × 835)

Dᴇsᴘɪᴛᴇ its name, the function of Christ's Hospital is given away by the group of schoolboys in their traditional long blue coats and yellow stockings shown under the arch in Lewis's drawing. Christ's Hospital was founded as a charity school on the site of London's dissolved Carthusian monastery in 1553. Despite improvements by Hawksmoor and others in the seventeenth and eighteenth centuries, its fabric in 1795 was essentially medieval and dilapidated. Lewis had been appointed surveyor to Christ's Hospital in 1792 and produced two designs 'for the uniform and gradual rebuilding of the hospital' in 1794 and 1795. In the latter year the governing body obtained an Act of Parliament allow-

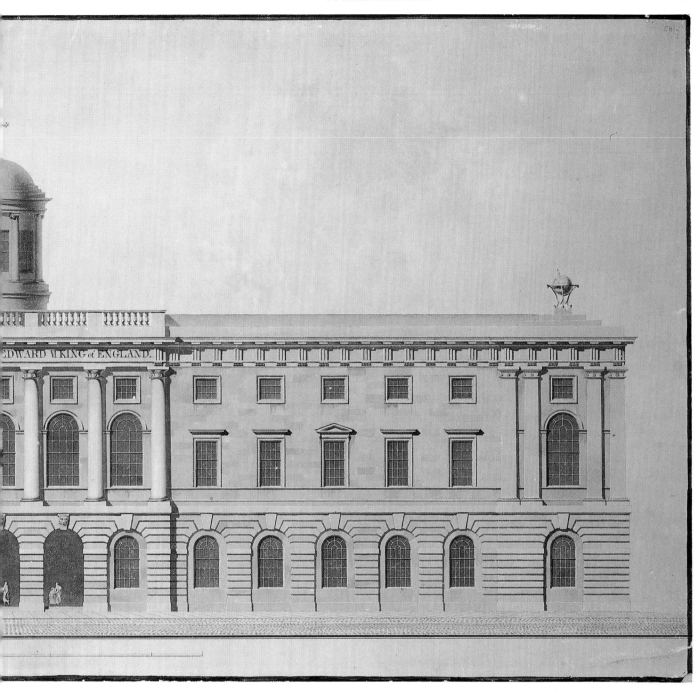

ing them to rebuild, but with war raging the 1790s were not a good time to raise money for such an ambitious project. It was only after the war, in 1820, that the scheme was revived, this time to the Gothic designs of John Shaw. It has been calculated that by 1837 £150,000 had been spent on the new school.

Lewis subsequently exhibited the designs at the Royal Academy in 1799 and 1800, and this drawing may have been made for that purpose. It is a particularly beautiful drawing highlighted with delicate washes.

Lewis showed a specific interest in designing large public buildings. At the start of his career he entered the competition for the design of the 540 foot-long St Luke's Lunatic Hospital in 1777, and he subsequently designed the new Bethlehem Hospital in Southwark, now the Imperial War Museum. He was also surveyor to Bridewell Hospital, but his main practice lay in country houses and villas.

Edward Blore 1787-1879
Design for the English School (now
the Modern School), Bedford
22 Perspective of the entrance front
with a cut-out flyleaf showing a low
retaining wall with lamp standards
and a street scene with figures in the
foreground, 1833-7
Watercolour, pen and sepia wash
(225 × 400)

B<small>LORE</small> began life not as an
architect but as a topographical
draughtsman, and it was through his
knowledge of accurate medieval details that he made the transition from
recorder to designer. Despite his lack
of training he soon gained the reputation of an architect whose estimates
could be relied on. His experience as
a topographical draughtsman stood
him in good stead, and his perspectives are always attractive. This
drawing was later adapted for engraving, perhaps to commemorate
the completion of the school, when
an additional strip of paper with the
street scene in a different hand was
pasted across it.

The Harpur Trust had been established in 1552 and was responsible
for a number of schools in Bedford.
In 1828 it was decided to unite four
different parts of the Trust, including
the English School, into one building. Preliminary designs by the surveyor of the Trust's London property
John Elger were felt to be functional
but unimpressive and a competition
was announced. A premium of £50
was offered but no guarantee was
given that the design would be used.
The competition was won by John
Wing, a Bedford architect, but in the
end it was decided to appoint
Edward Blore who had been employed by the Duke of Bedford on the
Market House at Woburn. He was
given Elger's and Wing's schemes
and provided a design uniting the
four elements in a single Gothic
building with a central tower. The
contract was for £13,730.

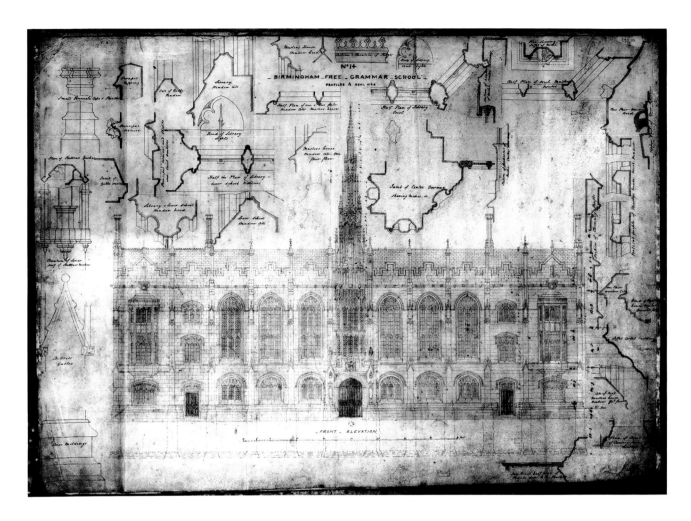

Charles Barry 1795-1860
Working drawing for King Edward
VI's School, Birmingham
23 Front elevation with profiles of
jambs and mouldings, 1835
Pen and wash (515 × 735)

Kᴵɴɢ Edward's School is another example of a new school building in the Gothic style erected as the result of the reform of a long-established institution but is principally of note as the first example of A.W.N. Pugin's collaboration with Charles Barry. This was to bear fruit a few years later at the Houses of Parliament. Barry's early years had been difficult, and he had been forced to enter successive competitions, often without success. Changing taste rendered many of the lessons gained on his Grand Tour redundant and on his return he concentrated on the study of Gothic architecture. He never found this particularly congenial and his most successful work was in his Italianate style.

At the time of the drawing Pugin was a young man of twenty-three whose extraordinary knowledge of Gothic architecture was used by other architects, including James Gillespie Graham, to provide authentic detail for their buildings. Barry turned to Pugin to provide appropriate details for his Gothic designs for King Edward's School. Their first recorded meeting with Barry was on 18 April 1835, and ten days later Pugin began working on drawings for King Edward's. He does not seem to have been satisfied with this work despite its Gothic details, and in the middle of working for Barry an uncharacteristic outburst in his diary declares: 'The present state of architecture is deplorable. Truth reduced to the position of an interesting but rare and curious relic.'

The school was demolished in 1936.

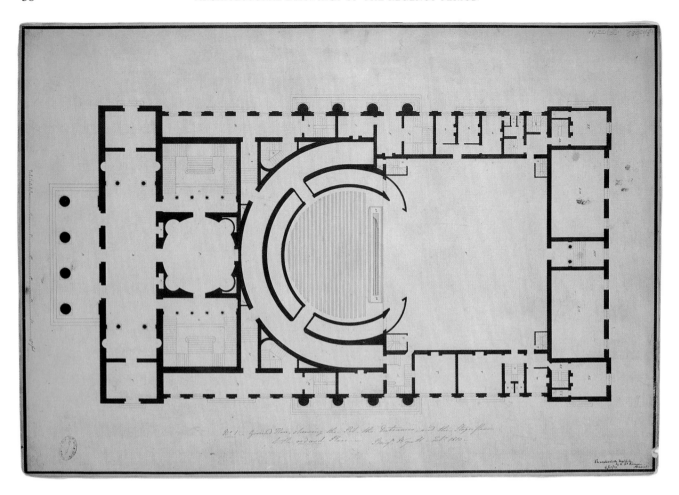

Benjamin Dean Wyatt 1775-c. 1855
Design for the Theatre Royal, Drury
Lane, Westminster, London
24 Ground floor plan, 1810
Pen and wash (450 × 655)

25 Front elevation, 1810
Pen and wash (475 × 655)

26 Longitudinal section, 1810
Pen and wash (430 × 655)

Benjamin Dean Wyatt was the
eldest son of James Wyatt. He did
not train as an architect but was sent
to Oxford and then to India. After
five years he returned to England in
1802, but it was only in 1809 that he
took up architecture. He made a
detailed study of theatres and was
well placed when a competition was
announced to rebuild the Theatre
Royal, Drury Lane which had been
destroyed by fire. Subsequently, he
countered accusations of plagiarism
made by his second cousin George
Wyatt with *Observations on the Design for the Theatre Royal, Drury
Lane, as Executed in the Year 1812.*

The competition was announced
in May 1811. The only well-known
entrant was William Wilkins and
Wyatt's design was chosen in October. On the twenty-ninth of that
month the foundation stone was laid,
and the theatre opened to the public
on 11 October 1812. Wyatt had put
great thought into all aspects of the
design, in particular into audibility,
the auditorium being round, and into
fire safety, with a brick shell round
the auditorium and staircases of
stone which could hold 1,528 people
at once in case of fire. The neo-
Palladian elevation (25) was not executed, probably for reasons of economy, but shows the influence of that
style even at this date.

Unfortunately, the new theatre
never made money, and the auditorium was reconstructed ten years
later. The present portico was added
in 1831, but the staircase survives.

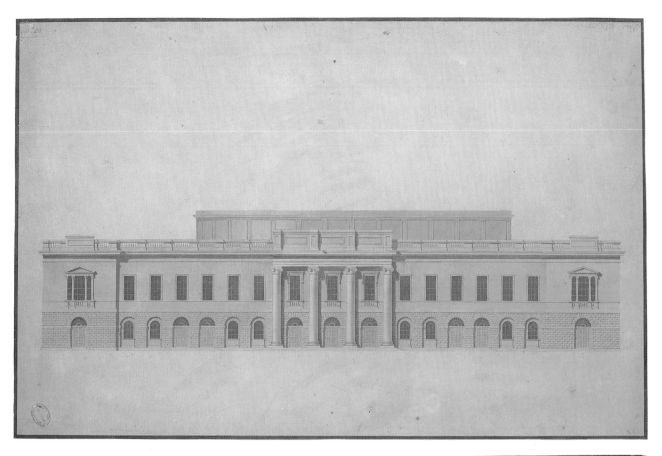

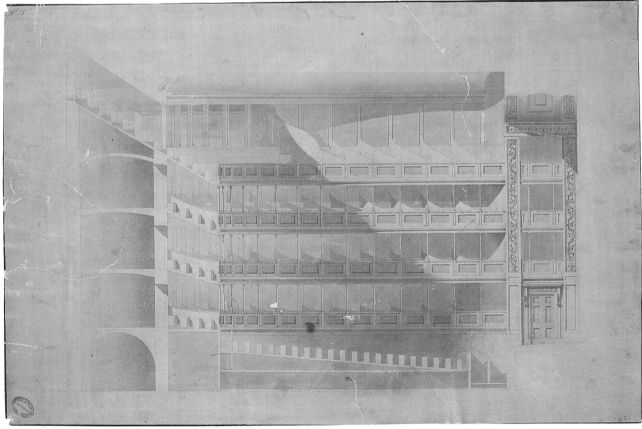

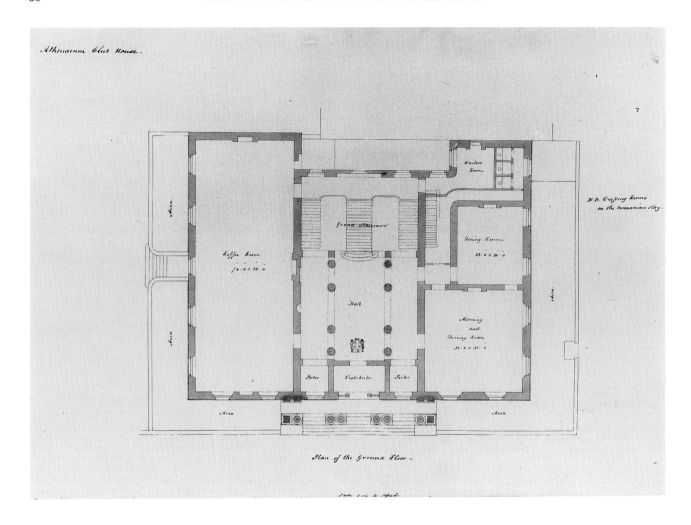

Decimus Burton 1800-1881
Record drawings by William Burn
1789-1870 of the Athenaeum Club,
Lower Regent Street, Westminster,
London
27 Ground floor plan, 1827-30
Pen and wash (335 × 515)

28 Front elevation, 1827-30
Pen and wash (335 × 510)

29 First floor plan, 1827-30
Pen and wash (355 × 515)

GENTLEMEN'S clubs were one of the most important social developments of the Regency period, moving away from being pure gambling or drinking haunts to well-equipped second homes with libraries, dining rooms, etc. The Athenaeum was established for literary and scientific men and followers of the arts ill-served by existing clubs. The total cost including furniture was £43,101. It was one of six London clubs included in a volume of measured drawings made by William Burn probably copied from the original drawings. This was presumably made in preparation for designing the New Club in Edinburgh in 1834.

Burton was the son of James Burton, the greatest speculative builder of his day, who was responsible for much of the Regent Street development. The Athenaeum was at the southern end of Regent Street and was supposed to look the same as the United Services Club across the street, but as Nash would not show Burton the drawings it differs significantly. The frieze, a copy of the Parthenon frieze, was a late addition to ensure the Athenaeum was not outshone by the United Services Club. An attic storey was added in 1889.

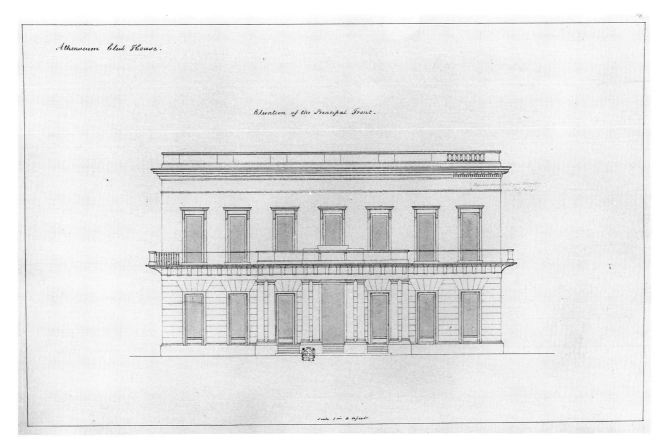

Athenaeum Club House.

Elevation of the Principal Front.

Scale 1 in. to 16 feet.

Athenaeum Club House.

Reading Room
43.4 x 30.0

Grand
Staircase

Landing

Balcony

Map Room.

Reading
Room.

Balcony

Note: The rooms over this Story are
Servants Sitting and Sleeping Rooms.

Library
100 x 30.

Balcony.

Plan of the Principal Story.

Scale of

John Goldicutt 1793-1842
Competition design for Fishmongers'
Hall, City of London
30 River elevation, 1830
Pencil and wash (265 × 300)

THE construction of a new London Bridge meant that the old Fishmongers' Hall overlooking the Thames had to be demolished. In August 1831 the Fishmongers' Company set aside £50,000 to finance a new hall and announced a competition for its design in *The Times*, *The Morning Chronicle* and *The Herald*. Premiums of £200, £150 and £100 were offered for the three best designs. The winner was Henry Roberts, a former assistant of Smirke's, but among the most attractive of the eighty-three entries (although it did not receive a premium) was that of John Goldicutt.

After training under Henry Hakewill and attending the Royal Academy schools where he won the silver medal in 1814, Goldicutt took advantage of the end of the Napoleonic Wars to study at the school of A. Leclere in Paris. He subsequently travelled to Rome where he was awarded a gold medal by the pope. On his return he settled in Hakewill's office, although apparently also practising independently, and seldom missed an opportunity to enter a competition.

Goldicutt's draughtsmanship is particularly impressive, perhaps showing the influence of his French training. He shared with C.R. Cockerell an ability to incorporate archaeological material in his designs, but failed to achieve the latter's success in translating novel architecture into executed buildings. His Fishmongers' design takes full advantage of its river site with a massive rusticated superstructure, perhaps inspired by Chambers' neighbouring Somerset House.

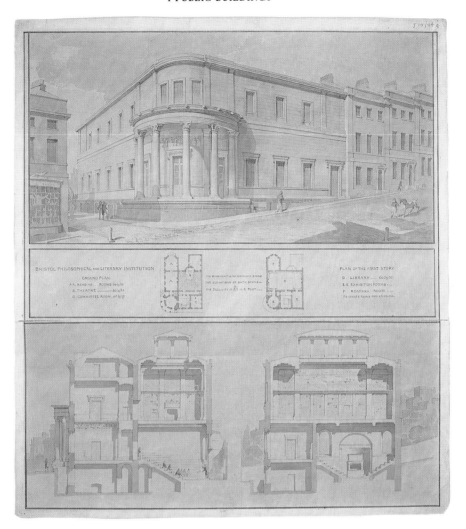

Charles Robert Cockerell
1788-1863
Design for the Bristol Philosophical
and Literary Institution
31 Plans of ground and first floors,
transverse and longitudinal sections
and perspective, 1821
Pencil and watercolour (510 × 460)

According to an inscription on the back of this drawing Cockerell gained the commission for the Bristol Institution thanks to John Harford who had employed John Nash to design Blaise Hamlet and was later to employ Cockerell to add a picture room to Blaise Castle.

The total cost of the work came to £11,251 9s, of which Cockerell was paid only £400, significantly less than the five per cent that would have been considered usual. The planning of the building on an awkward site was masterly, but Cockerell was not entirely happy with this early design, noting in his diary on 3 May 1822: 'cols look slender but graceful basemt remarkably well . . . on reflexion am convinced that the horizontal lines should have been avoided as the deformity of the descent more obvious than the perpendicular lines', and in June 1823 'my impression of the elevation always unfavourable in respect of Portico inharmoniously attached to the Buildg'.

This drawing was exhibited at the Royal Academy in 1821, but did not greatly impress the Academicians. When Cockerell sought election to the Royal Academy in 1823 the sculptor John Flaxman reported that the 'drawing of the buildg in Bristol disappointed them, the academicians, that it was little better than a shop front.' Nevertheless, the layout of the drawing with a perspective, two plans and two sections on one sheet is unusual for its date and shows an intelligent attempt to portray all the critical information about a building in a compact but attractive fashion.

The Institution later became a masonic hall and was gutted by bombing in 1940-1.

II THE COUNTRY HOUSE

Somewhat surprisingly, the years of the Napoleonic Wars saw the construction of some of the largest country houses ever built. High taxes were doubtless balanced by high grain prices thanks to the Continental blockade, but the profits of coal, industry and banking were also important. The 1790s were tight years. They had their share of large houses — Tyringham Hall, Buckinghamshire (1793), Fonthill Abbey, Wiltshire (1795), Dodington Park, Avon (1796), Ickworth, Suffolk (1796) — but they were relatively few. By comparison the first decade of the nineteenth century not only saw a significant number of new houses, but many of these were built on a vast scale: Belvoir Castle, Leicestershire (1801), for the Duke of Rutland; Stratton Park, Hampshire (1803), for Sir Francis Baring; Rosneath, Strathclyde (1803), for the Duke of Argyll; Grange Park, Hampshire (1805), for Henry Drummond; Sezincote, Gloucestershire (1805), for Sir Charles Cockerell (C.R. Cockerell's uncle) (57); Lowther Castle, Cumbria (1808), for the Earl of Lonsdale; Ashridge Park, Hertfordshire (1808), for the Earl of Bridgwater (41). The builders are a list of the great aristocracy mixed in with bankers and nabobs.

Land continued to exert its fascination over bankers, nabobs and others with new money in the years after Waterloo, and with the economy expanding rapidly their hands can be found in many new houses. James Balfour at Whittinghame

House, East Lothian (1817) was the son of a nabob (47-9). Peter Dixon at Holme Eden, Cumbria (1833) was the largest cotton manufacturer in Carlisle (46). These were also good years for agriculture, and so good years for the lesser landowner to rebuild: William Wyndham in 1814 at Dinton Park, Wiltshire (32-9); Edmund Bastard in about 1820 at Kitley House, Devon (42-4); Henry Preston in 1828 at Moreby Hall, North Yorkshire (45).

Balfour and Dixon both built afresh, as did George Eyre, son of the King's Printer, at the Warrens, Hampshire (58), in about 1805. With new money they could afford to. The gentry preferred to make use of what they had if they could. Kitley as rebuilt may have looked brand-new, but it was only refaced to make it more fashionable and reordered to make it more convenient (43-4). However, at Dinton, Wyndham, who had considered keeping his old house as offices and adding new reception rooms, was persuaded to start from scratch. For reasons of economy additions and remodelling were always more common than complete rebuilding, but these were frequent as each generation had to adapt the house to their habits of living. During the Regency, for instance, libraries became popular living rooms. They had not been common before and so at many houses like Quedgeley House, Gloucestershire (52) they had to be created.

Country-house living during the Regency was marked by increasing

informality within the family, but at the same time plans of houses became more compartmentalised, a development taken to an extreme in the Victorian house. At Whittinghame (48-9) the ground and first floor plans show that what appears from the outside to be a highly formal house was broken down into a series of self-contained sections. Most of the ground floor was given over to large reception rooms, but the west end formed a separate family wing centred round the bedroom of James Balfour and his wife Lady Eleanor, each of whom had their own dressing room with sitting room opening off it. Lady Eleanor's dressing room had a fixed bath. Above this, linked by a staircase, were two nurseries, presumably a day and a night nursery, with a further bedroom. None of these rooms communicated with the other bedrooms on the first floor. All bedrooms except one had dressing rooms, and were approached by the handsome main staircase, with a further lesser staircase for the servants.

Whittinghame (48) and Kitley (42) both had the family bedroom on the ground floor. At Kitley this was in a charming bay-windowed room, linked to the library by a domed ante-room, with a small dressing room and its own water closet. Whittinghame was also well served for water closets, with two for James and Lady Eleanor Balfour and one for the children. But all the other bedrooms were on the first floor and it became increasingly uncommon to have any ground-floor bedrooms.

The various designs for Dinton show the number of offices required by a medium-sized country house, although the full complement of offices shown in the presentation drawing (38) were reduced in the final design (37). In the presentation drawing a handful of offices were in the body of the house — the servants' hall, with a dressing room with sink off it, the butler's pantry with a small bedroom and plate room — but most of them were round a separate court. This comprised kitchen, scullery and pantry and larder, wash house, laundry and brew house. There were also separate privies for maids and men servants, a store for the brew house's malt and hops, a shed for cleaning shoes and knives, a tool shed, wood shed and coal shed, not forgetting the pig shed.

There are no basement offices at

Dinton, Whittinghame or Lough Crew (50); all the offices were pushed to the back part of the house or out into servants' wings. By 1834 when Earl de Grey built Wrest Park, Bedfordshire, the offices covered as large an area as the house, although they are deliberately low so that the house seems to rise surrounded only by walls.

Dinton is still an essentially Palladian villa with its central portico and tripartite facade (35). It represents the last gasp of the style, and looks back to the late work of Wyatville's uncle James Wyatt. Smirke and Cockerell, who belong to the next generation, attempted to move the classical country house beyond the Palladian model. For Smirke the answer lay in stripping classicism down to its bare essentials, removing virtually every vestige of the orders and relying on the cubic massing of

the house, as at Whittinghame (47). Cockerell was fascinated by the orders, of which he had made a detailed study on his Grand Tour, and he used them in novel combinations to great effect. Sadly, he only built three new houses.

But despite Smirke's and Cockerell's efforts to create new and original classical country houses the years after Waterloo were marked by an increasing drift towards Gothic, Elizabethan and Tudor architecture. Early examples like G.S. Repton's Kitley (44) of about 1820 still hark back to eighteenth-century Gothic, although with an increasingly accurate grasp of detail. Anthony Salvin's Moreby of 1828 is still essentially symmetrical (45), but by the time John Dobson designed Holme Eden in 1833 asymmetry had prevailed (46).

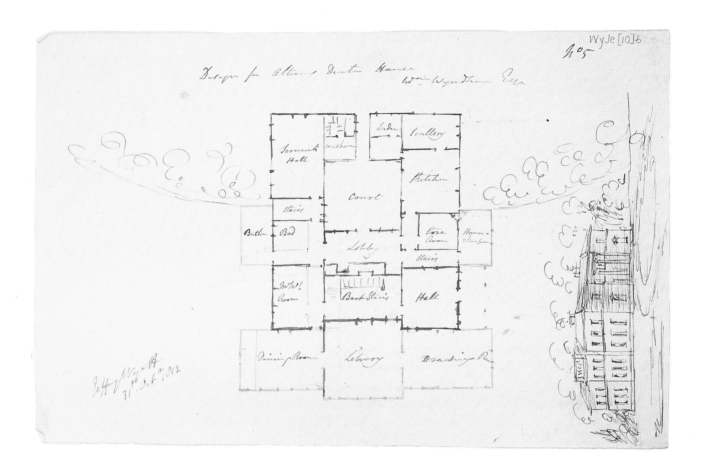

WILLIAM Wyndham succeeded to the Dinton estate in 1782 at the age of about 13, but it was not until 1812 that he decided to rebuild the H-shaped, probably seventeenth-century house that he had inherited. When the estate was acquired by his namesake, William Wyndham, the second son of Sir William Wyndham of Norrington, in 1689 it was not large, but it had been steadily extended during the later eighteenth and early nineteenth centuries through the acquisition of neighbouring blocks of land. Wyndham served as high sheriff of Wiltshire in 1814, and the rebuilding of Dinton Park was probably a seal on the family's county status.

For architectural guidance Wyndham relied heavily on the advice of his uncle John Wyndham, vicar of Corton in Somerset, who was clearly experienced in building matters, giving detailed advice on the practicalities of building and commenting on the drawings. It is uncertain why Wyatville was chosen as architect. The seventy-five drawings for Dinton, which come from the estate office there, allow us to trace the development of the rebuilding from the first tentative ideas, through alternative proposals, accepted plans and working drawings to its conclusion.

Dinton remained in the hands of the Wyndham family until 1940 when it was handed to the National Trust. It is now let as a conference centre.

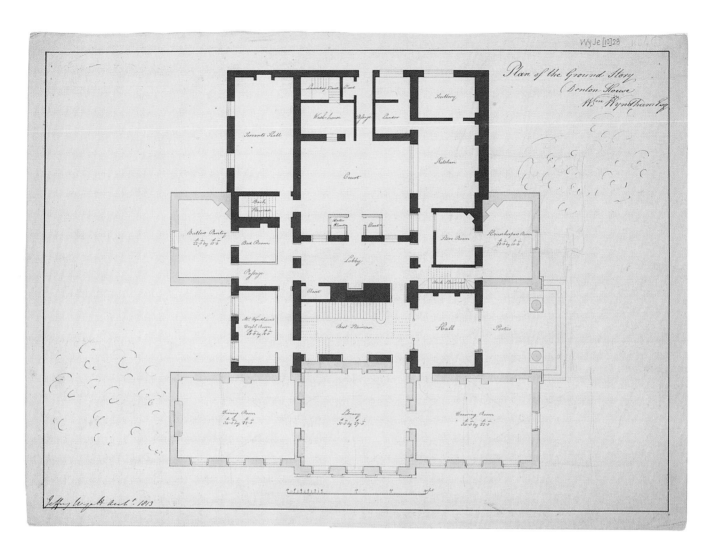

Sir Jeffry Wyatville 1766-1840
Design for Dinton Park, Wiltshire
33 Ground plan, 1813
Pen and coloured washes
(355 × 490)

WYATVILLE's first proposals for Dinton Park included the possibility of remodelling the existing house, so of the five sketch plans he made, two suggest ways of adding a new front while keeping the existing house as offices. Two of the sketches are dated 12 October 1812, and were probably made while Wyatville was at Dinton. The drawings, done crudely in pen, show rough outlines, with the existing work drawn out in black and the additions in pink.

One of the sketches, No. 5 (32), suggested adding a three-room front, with a dining room, library and drawing room, while a new entrance with a portico-in-antis was to be formed on the side elevation. A simple perspective on the same drawing shows an austere elevation. This scheme was seriously considered and the plan was drawn up neatly to scale once Wyatville had returned to his office (33). Again the old work is shown in black and the additions in pink, with timber walls coloured yellow and joinery, such as the library book shelves and dining-room sideboard, in brown. The scheme was not accepted and instead it was decided to build afresh, but the basic plan of the new house owes much to the plan here.

Sir Jeffry Wyatville 1766-1840
Design for Dinton Park, Wiltshire
34 Ground plan and front elevation,
1813
Pencil (415 × 260)

35 Front elevation, 1813
Pen and watercolour (345 × 480)

36 Front elevation, 1813
Pencil (315 × 510

THESE three drawings show Wyatville working through the final design of the south front, with the presentation drawing (35) carefully delineated in watercolour and signed *Jeffry Wyatt Archt. 1813*. Each drawing differs slightly. In 34 Wyatville originally considered using a giant baseless Doric order, but then added in volutes to suggest an Ionic order. The drawing also has pilasters on the returns and marked dormer windows. In 36 the Ionic columns have been drawn in but the pilasters have gone and the dormers are less obtrusive. Finally, in 35 the dormers have been removed altogether, the cornice is less austere, the first-floor windows have been dropped, a platband has been added and the plinth on which the house was sitting has been removed.

Dinton shows Wyatville in the most restrained late classical manner of his uncle James Wyatt. The design is very similar to that for Woodfold Hall, Lancashire, of 1798 on which he would have worked during his last year in James Wyatt's office. Ornament has been pared away to an absolute minimum, and even the columns of the giant Ionic order are unfluted. A service wing to the left of the house, like that James Wyatt had used at Dodington Park, Avon, was to be disguised by shrubbery.

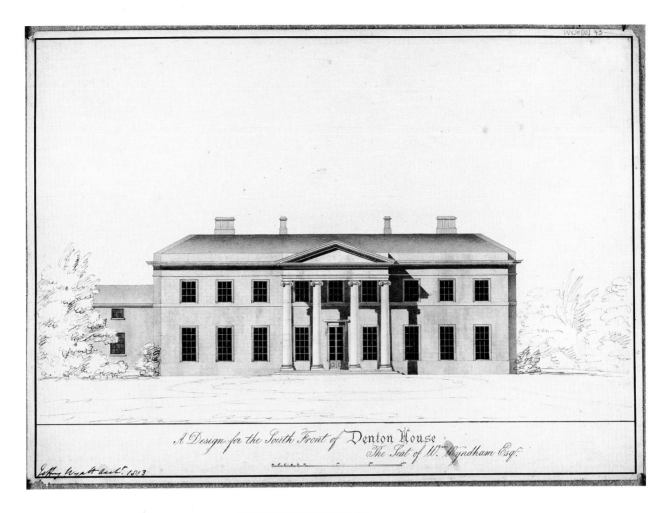

A Design for the South Front of Denton House
The Seat of Wm. Wyndham Esqr.

Jeffry Wyatt Archt. 1813

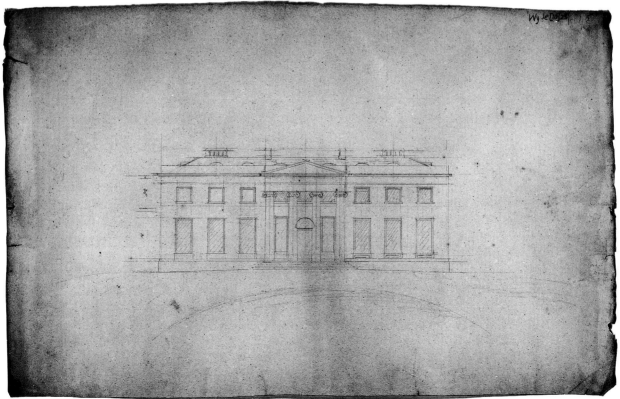

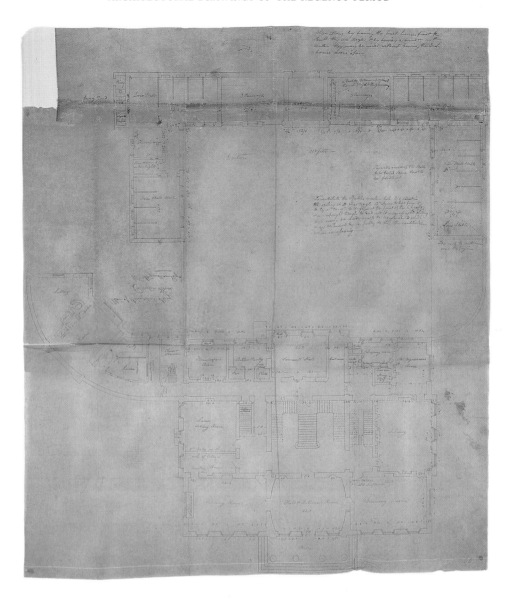

Sir Jeffry Wyatville 1766-1840
Design for Dinton Park, Wiltshire
37 Ground plan, *c.*1814
Pen on tracing paper (585 × 510)

38 Ground plan, 1813
Pen and wash (480 × 710)

39 Ground plan, 1814
Pen, pink and yellow washes
(545 × 760)

THESE three ground plans of Dinton show different stages in the design process. Number 38 is a presentation drawing, to accompany 35. This was the final design for William Wyndham to approve. After the long series of preparatory sketches the plan of the house was accepted with only minor alterations — a housekeeper's room was created — but the idea of an office court was replaced by a smaller wing. While 38 is for Wyndham, 39 is a working drawing, with all the dimensions carefully added. Finally, 37, which is presum-ably a copy of another drawing as it is on tracing paper, shows the house as built, with the kitchen now in the wing, and with the stables drawn in. In 39 the existing stables had been blocked in.

The stabling is extensive, with six coach houses, nineteen stalls, a harness room and two loose stalls or boxes. Loose boxes were a novelty, originally appearing in racing stables in the late eighteenth century. Wyatville was among the first architects to introduce them to country houses.

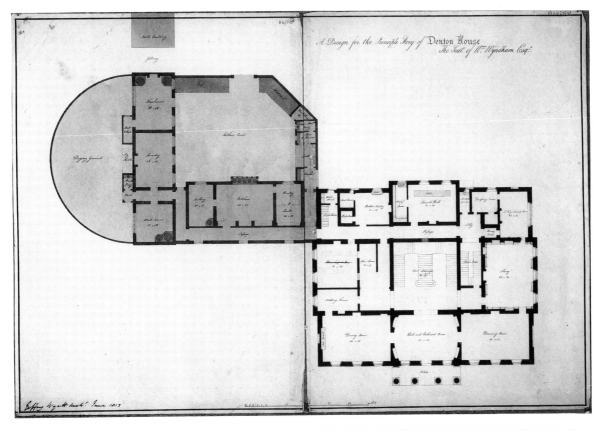

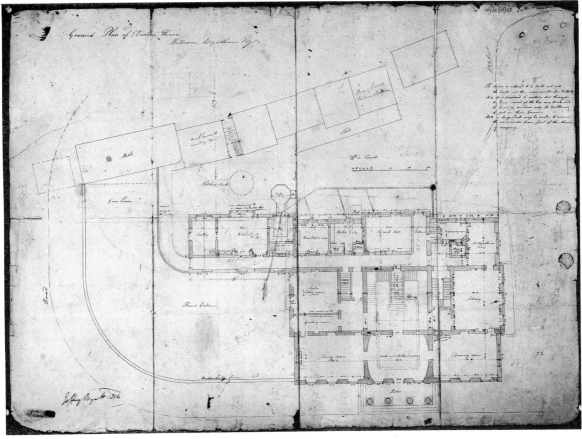

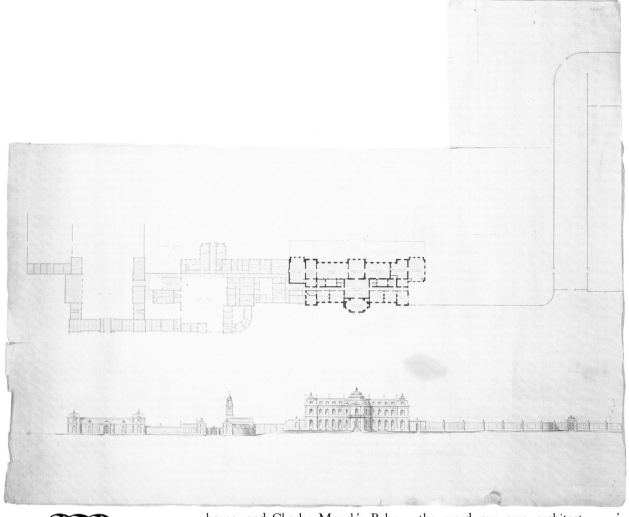

Thomas Philip de Grey, Earl de Grey 1781-1859
Design for Wrest Park, Bedfordshire
40 Plan of the house and offices and elevation of the entrance front, 1834-9
Pen and coloured washes
(640 × 810)

Aᴠᴛᴇʀ the numerous amateur architects of the eighteenth century, few are to be found during the Regency, but these show considerable originality. Thomas Hope with his Grecian style was the most famous, but Charles Hanbury Tracy's Toddington was an important Gothic house, and Charles Monck's Belsay took the Greek Revival to its extreme, while de Grey's use of the style of Louis XV at Wrest was without parallel. De Grey had architecture in his blood. He was born Thomas Robinson, and his father, the 2nd Lord Grantham, had also been an amateur architect. On succeeding to the Weddell estate at Newby Hall in Yorkshire in 1802 he changed his name to Weddell and added a dining room on the north side of the house, his first exercise in architecture. On the death of his maternal aunt Amabel, Countess de Grey, in 1833 he inherited Wrest Park and the earldom. Again he changed his name, but this time he completely rebuilt his new house.

'I was strictly and in every sense of the word my own architect ... ' wrote de Grey. 'I had my French books always under my hand [and] refered to them for authority whenever I could find anything to suit me.' For his working drawings de Grey relied on 'a Mr Brown, who had been Nash's clerk', and he employed James Clepham as his executant architect. Clepham had earlier acted in the same capacity for another amateur, Thomas Liddell. De Grey was a competent draughtsman and signed his drawings with a monogrammed G. This drawing is half of a long design on two sheets of paper, the other half only showing garden walls and a hothouse.

Wrest is now a college of agricultural engineering.

John Buckler 1770-1851
Topographical view of Ashridge
Park, Hertfordshire
41 Interior perspective of the stair-
case hall, 1813
Pencil and sepia wash (500 × 360)

THE Regency was a period when the connection between the topographical artist and the architect was close, with the one slipping easily into the role of the other. Buckler was a topographical draughtsman rather than an architect, although he was said to have been articled to C.T. Cricklow, a Southwark architect. At the end of his life he calculated that he had made over thirteen thousand sketches all over the country, particularly of medieval buildings. Buckler also worked on commission for private patrons, illustrating books, such as Colt Hoare's *Wiltshire*, or recording their houses. His drawings could easily be perspectives drawn by an architect to persuade his client to build.

The Earl of Bridgwater had inherited Ashridge in 1803, together with substantial estates in Hertfordshire, Buckinghamshire, Shropshire and Yorkshire from his cousin the 3rd Duke of Bridgwater. He began to remodel the house in 1808 and commissioned Buckler to record his work twice, once in 1813 on the death of the original architect James Wyatt, and again in 1822 when the building had been finished by Jeffry Wyatville.

Ashridge was typical of the very large, Gothic houses which were built during the first decades of the nineteenth century and show the great wealth of members of the aristocracy. Robert Smirke's Lowther

The Staircase at Ashridge

Castle in Cumbria of 1806-11 and Eastnor Castle, Herefordshire, built for the 2nd Lord Somers in 1812-20 are other examples, but the greatest of them all was Wyatville's remodelling of Windsor Castle for George IV from 1824 to 1840 at a cost of well over £1 million.

Ashridge is now a management college.

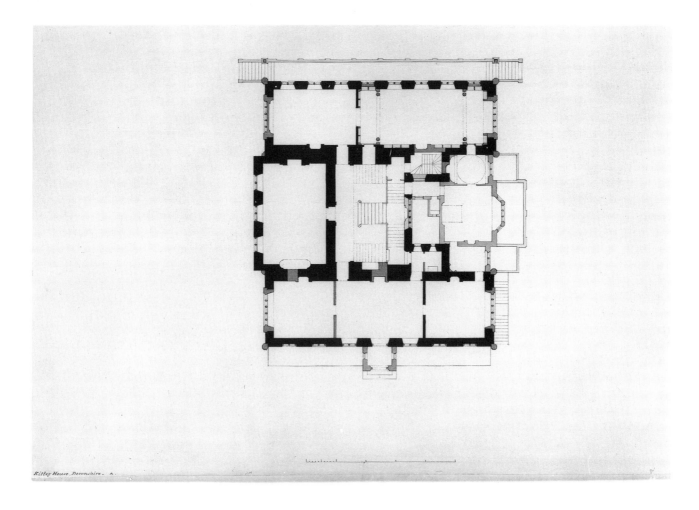

Kitley House Devonshire - A -

George Stanley Repton 1786-1858
Design for Kitley House, Devon
42 Ground floor plan showing
alterations, *c.* 1820-5
Pen and grey and yellow washes
(360 × 510)

43 Perspective of west front before
alteration, *c.* 1820-5
Pen and wash (365 × 535)

44 Perspective of west front after
alteration, *c.* 1820-5
Pen and wash (365 × 535)

G.S. REPTON, the landscape de-

signer Humphry Repton's youngest
son, was a pupil of John Nash and
became in time his chief assistant,
earning £1,500 a year. Kitley was his
first substantial commission after
leaving Nash's office, and the first in
a significant series of houses in the
West Country. Repton had learnt the
importance of good presentation
drawings from his father, and emulated his technique of preparing a
drawing with a flap showing the
building first as it was and then as it
could be. Unlike his father's red
books with their coloured drawings,
Repton's drawings are done in an
effective grey wash. The old fabric is
shown in black with the alterations in
grey and the joinery in yellow.

Edmund Bastard, who succeeded
to the Kitley estate in 1816, was an
amateur of the picturesque and of
horticulture. A creek of the Yealm
estuary was dammed to create a
suitable setting for Kitley. The house
he inherited was an attractive early
eighteenth-century remodelling of a
sixteenth-century structure. Bastard
called on Repton to recase it in
fashionable Elizabethan dress and to
rearrange the interior, but major
structural alteration was kept to a
minimum. For stylistic detail Repton
turned to his knowledge of sixteenth-
century East Anglian architecture. In
particular details can be paralleled
with Helmingham Hall, Suffolk,
which Nash had restored about 1800.

Anthony Salvin 1799-1881
Design for Moreby Hall, North
Yorkshire
45 Perspective of the entrance front,
1828-32
Watercolour (475 × 700)

SALVIN was to be one of the most prolific of Victorian architects, but Moreby Hall, which was one of his first houses, shows him still designing in a style comparable with that of G.S. Repton (44). Although Charles Eastlake listed Moreby as an early example in his *A History of the Gothic Revival* (1872), the house remains essentially symmetrical. Salvin would soon move away from this reliance on symmetry to create a more recognisably Victorian style.

Henry Preston for whom Salvin built Moreby was a member of a long-established landowning family, although one with strong links with commerce in Leeds. It may be that he was inspired to rebuild the late seventeenth-century classical house at Moreby in the Elizabethan style to stress the fact that he was no parvenu.

This perspective was exhibited at the Royal Academy in 1828, the first of Salvin's designs to be so. James Deason was later employed by Salvin to draw his perspectives, but it is not clear whether he had joined Salvin's office in 1828.

Three years after designing Moreby Salvin was given the commission for Harlaxton Hall in Lincolnshire, the nearest that the nineteenth century came to an Elizabethan prodigy house.

John Dobson 1787-1865
Design, drawn possibly by
J.W. Carmichael 1800-1868, for
Holme Eden, Cumbria
46 Perspective of the south-east
front, 1833
Watercolour (275 × 455)

Dobson, who lived in Newcastle, was one of several Regency architects with the talent to establish themselves up in London but who made the decision to settle in a provincial capital. Initially he did not find it easy as the idea of a professional architect, rather than an architect-builder like his former master David Stephenson, was novel in the North. When he set himself up he was the only such architect apart from Ignatius Bonomi between York and Edinburgh. In time it proved a wise decision, for the first half of the nineteenth century were boom years in the North-East, and Dobson built up an enormous practice, being involved with sixty churches, a hundred houses and innumerable public buildings.

Holme Eden was built for Peter Dixon, the largest cotton manufacturer in Carlisle who had mills in Manchester, Carlisle and nearby at Warwick Bridge. The firm had expanded greatly in the 1820s and early 1830s and the family was at the height of its local influence. The house was built in a slightly simpler form than is shown here.

Dobson must have learnt the importance of attractive watercolours from John Varley who had taught him, and when his practice grew so extensive that he did not have time to make highly finished perspectives himself he employed J.W. Carmichael to do so and this drawing may be by him.

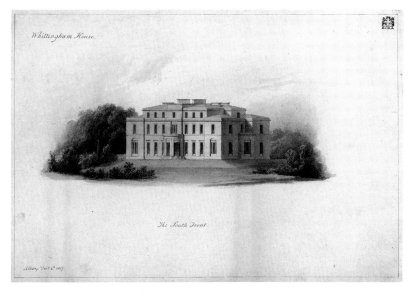

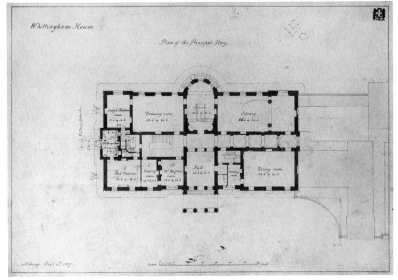

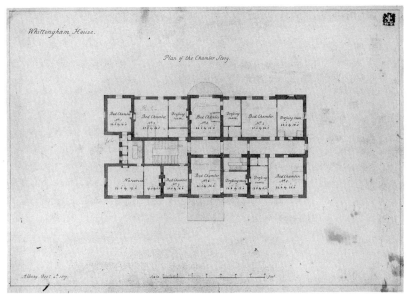

Sir Robert Smirke 1780-1867
Design for Whittinghame House, East Lothian
47 Perspective of the garden front, 1817
Watercolour (255 × 360)

48 Ground floor plan, 1817
Pen and wash (255 × 360)

49 First floor plan, 1817
Pen and wash (255 × 360)

ROBERT Smirke was among the most successful of all Regency architects. He rose swiftly to the top of his profession, becoming one of the three architects attached to the Board of Works at the age of thirty-three. The other two were Soane and Nash. He was involved with nearly fifty public buildings, over a score of churches and nearly sixty houses, died worth £90,000, and at the height of his career was rumoured to refuse commissions worth less than £10,000.

Although his Covent Garden Theatre of 1808 was the first pure Greek Revival building erected in the capital, Smirke's most interesting work was in his cubic style, which Pugin described as 'the New Square Style of Mr Smirke', where he tried to strip away classical detail and rely primarily on massing. The most important example of this was the Royal College of Physicians in Trafalgar Square, now Canada House, but it can also be seen in a series of country houses including Whittinghame.

Whittinghame was built for James Balfour, and was altered by Burn in 1827, and again in the 1890s. These drawings, dated 4 December 1817, are part of a set of six showing the two facades, basement, ground floor, first floor and attic. In simple attractive form they set out all the essential information for the prospective client.

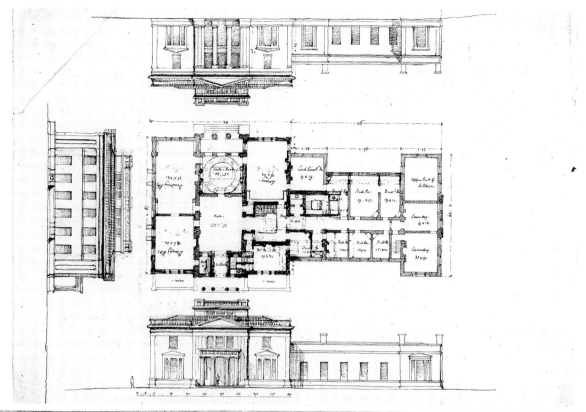

Charles Robert Cockerell
1788-1863
Design for Lough Crew, County
Meath, Ireland
50 Ground plan and three elevations,
1821-5
Pen (400 × 530)

51 Elevation, 1821-5
Pencil (40 × 195)

LOUGH Crew was one of only three new country houses which Cockerell designed. It was built for J.L. Naper who had strong views on its design, sometimes conflicting with those of the architect. The extensive office wing was added in 1823-5. Despite the fact that materials and labour were twenty-five per cent cheaper than in England, the cost of the house totalled £22,000. After a fire in 1888 Lough Crew was rebuilt without the attic storey, but was destroyed by another fire *c.* 1965.

The house established Cockerell as a master of the most austere phase of the Greek Revival and owes much to Sir Robert Smirke. Cockerell studied under Smirke for a year in 1809 before setting out for Greece and Turkey. In 1824 he confessed that 'I shall never get entirely out of Smirke's manner'. But even before Lough Crew was finished Cockerell began to regret the lack of movement and shadow. His later works achieve a more successful synthesis of classical detail.

The two drawings are typical of Cockerell's loose drawing style and admirably show how he developed his architectural ideas through drawing.

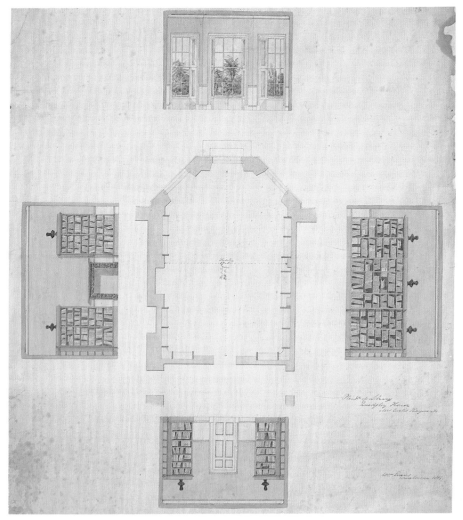

Thomas Evans *c.* **1784-1874**
Design for a library at Quedgeley
House, Gloucestershire
52 Plan and four wall elevations,
1819
Pen and watercolour
(400 × 455)

Libraries were popular rooms in
the Regency, often serving as the
main family living room. In his *Frag-
ments on the Theory and Practice of
Landscape Gardening*, published
three years before this drawing was
made, Humphry Repton included a
view of such a library full of people,

writing that 'the most recent custom
is to use the library as the general
living-room'. Many houses had existing rooms fitted up as libraries or
extensions with libraries added on.
This was what happened at
Quedgeley House where Albinia
Frances Hayward, who was married
to the Rev. John Curtis, added a
three-storeyed stucco extension to
the square late eighteenth-century
ashlar house she inherited on her
father's death in 1818.

Thomas Evans is an obscure
figure, obviously connected with
William Evans of Wimborne, County Surveyor of Dorset from 1824 to
1842. This drawing is signed *Wm
Evans/ Wimborne 1819*, and designs
for Ettington Hall, Warwickshire,

dated 1820-1, are partly signed by
William and partly by Thomas
Evans.

Evans's design shows how by the
early nineteenth century elegant,
clear draughtsmanship had spread
even to minor provincial architects,
whose drawings in the eighteenth
century were often crude. Evans exhibited at the Royal Academy in
1821 and 1823, but there is no evidence that he had received any training in London. Drawings of rooms
with the walls laid out flat on a single
sheet were standard eighteenth-
century practice.

Quedgeley House was sold by the
Curtis-Hayward family in 1939 and
subsequently divided into flats.

Joseph Bonomi 1739-1808
Design for the dining room at
Lambton Castle, County Durham
53 Interior perspective, 1800
Pen and watercolour (450 × 645)

Bonomi had been recruited in
Rome as a draughtsman by the
Adam brothers in 1767. He remained
in their office, forbidden under the
penalty of a £100 bond from produc-
ing any work of his own, until 1783
when he returned to Italy. This visit
was not a success and he returned

home the following year to establish
his own practice. Externally his work
is severe, but his interiors were often
sumptuous.

Bonomi was a very fine draughtsman, even his working drawings are
handsomely produced, but it is his
superb interior perspectives for
which he is chiefly famed. These, like
this one of the dining room at Lambton Castle, were often shown at the
Royal Academy, where he was probably the first architect to exhibit such
drawings. His work in the Adam
office is unclear, but it may be that
the view of the third drawing room at
Derby House in the second volume
of *The Works of Robert and James
Adam* (1779), which shows a similar

use of perspective, was drawn by
Bonomi.

Lambton Castle was not Bonomi's
happiest commission. A massive
scheme for a new house was rejected
and instead Bonomi made piecemeal
alterations which were interrupted by
the death of W.H. Lambton in 1797.
Further work was carried out after
Bonomi's death by his son Ignatius
Bonomi, but subsidence meant that
the house had to be largely rebuilt in
1860-2. Although the drawing makes
the room look very sparse, that is
probably intentional: a deliberate
contrast with the sumptuousness of
the reception rooms, not a record of a
half-finished commission.

Joseph Potter *c.* **1756-1842**
Design for Plas Newydd, Anglesey,
Gwynedd
54 Elevation, of a wall possibly in
the dining room, 1795-1823
Pen and coloured washes
(350 × 340)

POTTER was an architect and builder based in Lichfield who established a successful practice through the patronage of James Wyatt who used him as his executant architect in the Marches and Wales. He supervised Wyatt's alterations to Lichfield and Hereford Cathedrals in 1788-93 and 1790-3 and helped repair St Michael's Church, Coventry, in 1794. From 1795 he was involved at Plas Newydd on the Isle of Anglesey first carrying out Wyatt's alterations and then making his own designs. He became the established architect at Lichfield Cathedral, was County Surveyor of Staffordshire for forty-five years, and carried out a series of works for the Marquess of Anglesey, building new baths and assembly rooms at Caernarvon in 1822 and altering Beaudesert, Staffordshire, in 1826-31.

Potter's work was unexceptional, and this drawing is typical of the standard, well-produced designs turned out for simple rooms by a minor provincial architect. Its restraint is characteristic of the austerity of late eighteenth-century interiors which, though still using a classical vocabulary, have pared that down to a minimum. Thus the pilaster has no base and the cornice is a simple modillion one.

Henry Holland 1745-1806
Record drawing of a fireplace
and overmantel
55 Details *c.* 1801
Pen (375 × 260)

Few of Holland's papers survive because they seem to have been destroyed by his executor after his death, but three volumes of drawings of his are in the RIBA. These are not sketchbooks but record books into which Holland's original drawings were copied by his assistants for reference. This seems to have been common practice among leading architects, and was emulated by Soane who began his career as an assistant in Holland's office from 1772-8. Two of the volumes are for Carlton House, but the third volume, from which this drawing is taken, is for various buildings. Not all the drawings are inscribed and it may be that this is a copy of an unexecuted design.

Holland was of the same generation as James Wyatt, and his office was important in establishing the way in which Regency architects practised. One increasingly controversial aspect of Regency architectural practice was speculative building. Holland and Wyatt, like all the leading architects of the preceding generation, were heavily involved in speculative building. Holland took an eighty-nine acre site from Lord Cadogan in Chelsea which he developed. One of the great battles of the early nineteenth century was to separate the role of the architect from that of the builder so that he had no link with contracting.

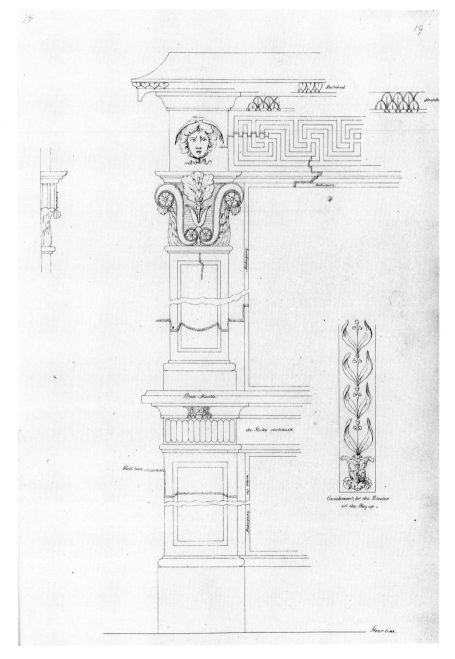

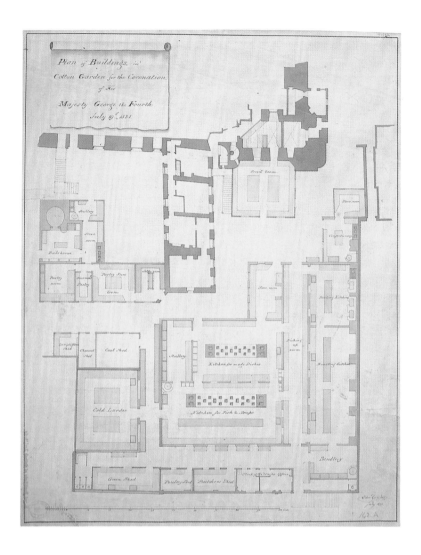

Edward Crocker c. 1757-1836
Design for kitchens in Cotton
Garden, Westminster, London,
erected for the coronation of
George IV
56 Plan, 1821
Pen and coloured washes
(570 × 450)

ALTHOUGH not strictly for a
country house, Crocker's drawing
demonstrates the workings of a kitch-
en on the grandest scale. It shows the
temporary kitchens built on a site
adjoining Westminster Hall to service the great coronation banquet of
George IV in 1821, the last for any
monarch. The drawing is carefully
colour-coded, enabling us to see what
was existing stonework (dark grey),
what was temporary brick (pink),
wood (brown); the cooking surfaces
(light grey); the heat-resistant areas
around the cooking surfaces (red);
basins (light blue); wooden surfaces
(ochre) and cold surfaces, probably
slate, (blue). In the centre are the two
kitchens for made dishes and fish, off
which are a roasting kitchen, boiling
kitchen, pastry room, jelly room,
confectionery room, pantries, store
rooms and numerous other rooms.

Crocker was an employee of the
Office of Works, into which he had
followed his father. He was a surveyor rather than an architect, and
his career culminated with the post
of Clerk of Works at Whitehall
which he held from 1818 until his
retirement at the age of 72 in 1829.
Although Westminster Hall lay within Soane's jurisdiction as one of the
three attached architects to the office
of works, he had prevaricated in
agreeing to organise the coronation
banquet and so the Surveyor-General
entrusted supervision of the Hall's
fitting up to Robert Browne, the
Assistant Surveyor-General, with
Crocker acting as Clerk of Works.

Thomas Daniell 1749-1840
Design for a bridge at Sezincote,
Gloucestershire
57 Perspective, c. 1810
Pen and watercolour
(210 × 305)

THOMAS Daniell and his nephew William achieved fame through their topographical drawings and paintings made in India from 1786 to 1793. They were among the first British artists to travel to India, and on their return home they published a set of 144 aquatints in six parts between 1795 and 1808 entitled *Oriental Scenery* at a cost of £210 a set. The RIBA holds a large number of preliminary drawings for these.

As the acknowledged expert on Indian architecture it was not surprising that Thomas Daniell was brought in to advise on the detailing of Sezincote, just as experts such as A.W.N. Pugin advised on the details of Gothic buildings. Sezincote was designed by S.P. Cockerell for his brother Sir Charles Cockerell who had made a substantial fortune in India. Humphry Repton advised on the garden and Daniell designed the farm and garden buildings as well as helping with the detailing of the house. The bridge, which served the main drive and stood at the head of the water garden, was executed much as it is shown here, although with two bulls instead of one.

Sezincote is typical of the stylistic eclecticism of Regency architecture, although Indian architecture was always exceptional.

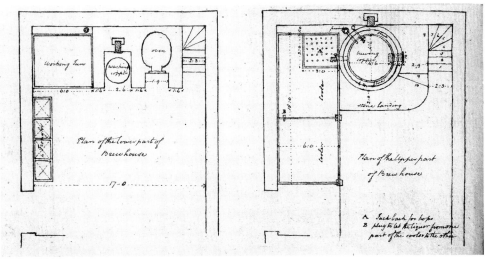

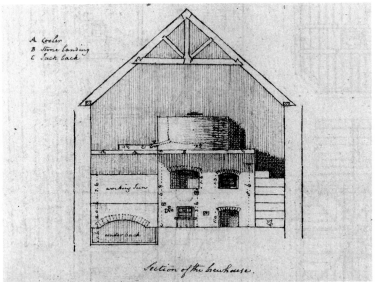

John Nash 1752-1835
Record drawing by George Stanley
Repton 1786-1858 of the brew house
at the Warrens, Bramshaw,
Lyndhurst, Hampshire
58a Two plans, *c.* 1805
Pen (95 × 160)

58b Section, *c.* 1805
Pen (95 × 160)

REPTON worked in Nash's office
from about 1801 to about 1820, and
the notebook from which this draw-

ing is taken is watermarked 1798,
soon after Nash's return to London.
Like the Holland drawing (55), this is
a record drawing made by an assistant, not by the architect himself. But
whereas Holland's was made for the
office records, Repton's was probably
for his own information, an attempt
to build up a stock of examples for
later use. Charles Cockerell noted in
his diary in 1824 that Nash recommended his pupils to make hand
drafts of all the works going on,
which they did first thing in the
morning, and which helped them to
acquire 'wonderful facility'. Repton's
notebook mostly consists of records
of minor buildings, particularly

cottages.

Warrens had been bought by
George Eyre in 1798. His father, who
had lived in Clapham, had held the
patent as King's Printer and served as
High Sheriff in 1780. In time Eyre
managed to consolidate a considerable property and to establish himself
in the gentry, serving as Verderer of
the New Forest, JP for Wiltshire and
Hampshire and High Sheriff of Wiltshire. He employed Nash to rebuild
Warrens for him around 1805. This
drawing of a brew house is a useful
record of the sort of domestic office
essential in every substantial country
house.

John Adey Repton 1775-1860
Design for a lodge
59 Perspective, n.d.
Pen and wash (205 × 290)

J.A. REPTON was Humphry Repton's eldest son. Like his younger brother George, John served in the office of John Nash, although he had been apprenticed to William Wilkins. When Humphry Repton and Nash fell out in 1802, partly because Nash gave no credit to the role played by J.A. Repton in his designs, J.A. Repton entered into a partnership with his father, carrying out the architectural side while the older man laid out the gardens and parks. J.A. Repton was deaf from birth; after the death of his father his practice largely ceased and he devoted himself to antiquarian pursuits.

Repton's draughtsmanship is very hard to distinguish from that of his brother, both using the same technique of grey wash vignettes. It is unclear whether this is a design for an executed building, but it is probable as other lodges in the same series can be identified.

Nash was an important figure in the origin of the cottage style, his most famous examples being at Blaise Hamlet, built in 1810-11. The style was inspired by the vernacular architecture of the South of England, and in particular by cottages portrayed by contemporary painters. This lodge, with its thatched roof and small, asymmetrical leaded windows set in a quiet glade could easily be taken from such a painting. The corollary to such cottages designed for domestics and workmen were cottage ornés, elaborate villas dressed up to look like simple cottages (80).

James Wyatt 1746-1813
Design for stables at White Lodge,
Richmond Park, Richmond, London
60 Plans, elevations and
sections, 1801
Pen and coloured washes
(495 × 385)

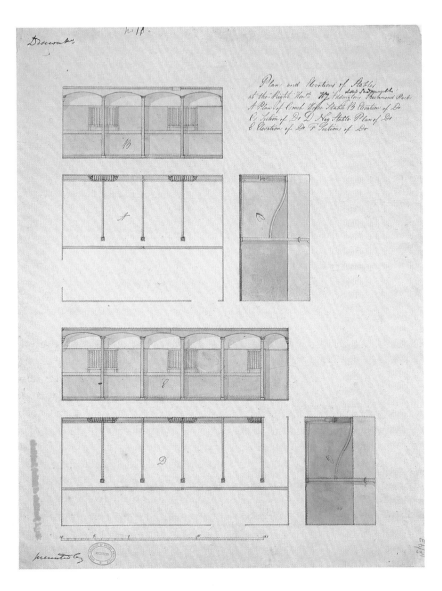

IN MANY ways James Wyatt was the prototype of the Regency architect, although he first sprang to fame in 1769 when he designed the Pantheon in London. Prodigiously gifted, he could design in any style he wished and built up an enormous practice which was responsible for over a hundred country houses. But whereas most Regency architects are marked by unrelenting hard work and efficiency, Wyatt failed to organise his practice effectively, and William Porden told Farington in 1806 that he lost £2,000 to £3,000 a year 'from mere neglect in respect of order in his accounts'.

Wyatt's work at White Lodge arose from his position as Surveyor-General of the Office of Works, as it sat in Richmond Park, a royal park. It was extended and remodelled for the Ranger of Richmond Park, the 1st Viscount Sidmouth, in 1801-6. This drawing of the coach house and nag stalls in the stables would undoubtedly have been made by one of Wyatt's clerks. The basic design of the interior of stables had not changed since the seventeenth century, but the arrival of the loose box then being introduced in racing stables was shortly to revolutionise stable design.

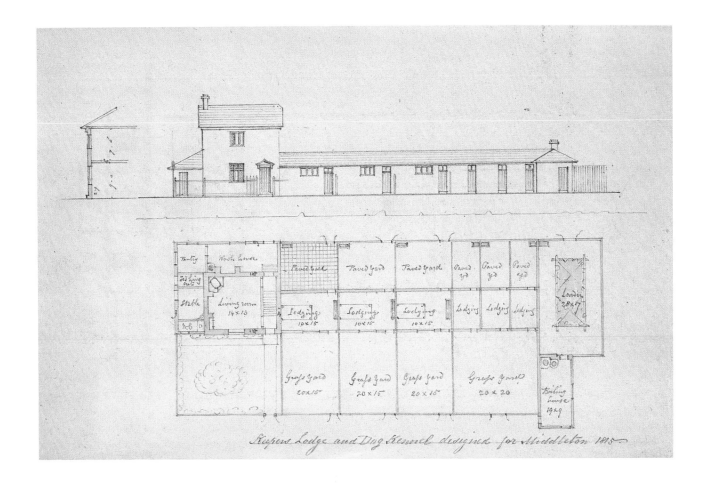

Thomas Cundy 1765-1825
Record drawing of the keeper's lodge
and dog kennel at Middleton Park,
Oxfordshire
61 Plan and elevation, 1815
Pen, sepia pen, pencil and
coloured washes
(120 × 200)

Hunting was the preferred activity of the gentry and aristocracy in the country, and the Regency saw marked changes in the pattern of hunting as improved breeding of horses and hounds led to faster chases with more horses and larger packs. This spurred the revolution in stable design initiated in racing stables, and probably also led to improved kennels for the hounds.

Cundy made numerous designs for Middleton Park for the 5th Earl of Jersey. He altered and refaced the house, and built new stables, kennels, lodges and a parsonage. This drawing comes from a small volume of record drawings kept by Cundy's son who succeeded to the practice. It not only recorded executed designs, often with details of their cost, but schemes that were superseded or put aside. This drawing anticipates later nineteenth-century kennels with their series of lodgings, each with their grass and paved yards. At one end is the small huntsman's cottage, at the other the boilinghouse and larder. The design was not executed. A simpler drawing is annotated showing that it was built in 1815.

Cundy was the eldest son of a minor Cornish gentleman but fell out with his father, and after apprenticeship to a builder in Plymouth he entered S.P. Cockerell's office as clerk of works. He educated himself by private study and at the Royal Academy, and set himself up as an architect and builder in Pimlico, eventually being appointed surveyor to Lord Grosvenor's estates in Belgravia and Pimlico.

III SMALLER HOUSES

THE rapid growth of the middle classes during the Regency was paralleled by the number of smaller detached houses built on the outskirts of towns and cities and in villages. The newly found professional status of architects meant that a suburban villa was something to which a successful architect might aspire. Through talent and hard work John Soane established himself as one of the country's leading architects during the 1790s, and by 1800 he could afford to buy Pitzhanger Manor at Ealing. This he swiftly altered, keeping an existing wing but building a substantial new block.

Such houses or villas are marked by the fact that they had little land, sometimes no more than a garden. Little Grove in East Barnet, bought by Frederick Cass in 1827, came with forty-nine acres which allowed J.B. Papworth to design a miniature landscape park complete with shelter belts, clumps of trees and an ornamental lake (63), but that was unusual. It was more common for villas to be included in an estate made up of a number of houses set in a communal park. Nash's Regent's Park was the archetype for this, but the germ of the idea could be seen at the Casina in Dulwich (72). Here Nash had been working in partnership with Humphry Repton, designing a house for which Repton laid out the grounds. These stretched down to an ornamental canal which was intended to form a feature for a number of similar villas. Nothing came of this and only eight of the twenty-six proposed villas for Regent's Park were ever built, but the idea was influential. The Calverley estate at Tunbridge Wells, where James Hakewill (Henry's brother) tried to persuade G.W. Aylmer to build a villa (76), was being laid out on similar lines by Decimus Burton who had been responsible for designing most of the villas in Regent's Park.

Regency villas always aimed to minimise their appearance of size, and in the design attention was focused on the family rooms which were made to look as if they stood alone, with the servants' wing, which often equalled the main block in size, hidden away, sheltered by trees. This is well shown in Hakewill's design for G.W. Aylmer (76). Hakewill submitted two designs, both follow much the same layout for the family rooms, but in one the offices are placed under the house in a basement, while in the other they stretch back in an independent wing. At £5,000, the first was £1,000 cheaper; but the latter was preferred. As Soane had said in his lectures: 'the more important Offices of a Villa should never be sunk entirely underground; either from a desire to obtain great compactness, or from a too strict regard for economy. Many inconveniences are to be apprehended, such as smells from the Kitchen and Scullery, and noise from the Servants Hall.' By 1811 the idea of a villa with offices in symmetrical wings like that at Largs (74) was definitely old-fashioned.

In layout Regency villas were scaled-down versions of full-blown country houses. Hakewill's villa compares well with Sir Jeffry Wyatville's Dinton Park (38). The same essential rooms are there: drawing room, dining room, library and study, all grouped round a central staircase. All that is missing is a large hall – which in the Hakewill design is reduced to a narrow passage – and the ladies' sitting room. The same is true of the offices, with both houses having a butler's pantry, housekeeper's room, servants' hall, kitchen, scullery and pantry with larder opening off it.

Papworth's Little Grove is unusually formal in its layout, with offices in a new wing matching the drawing room wing, but that is because he was remodelling an existing mid-eighteenth century house (67). One particularly interesting development at Little Grove is the first incipient signs of a specifically male part of the house. In the new wing is the butler's pantry, the china closet and a water closet, but also a gentlemen's room and a billiards room. The idea of a male preserve was to be characteristic of Victorian houses. Again, the main rooms at Little Grove are the drawing room, dining room and library, although the size of the original house meant that there was also room for an entrance hall, an ante-room between the hall and the drawing room, and a breakfast room. Dr Brown's house, Largs, was old-fashioned in having a parlour rather than a drawing room and a bedroom on the ground floor (75). It must also have had the kitchens in the basement.

Villas were well suited to the multiplicity of styles thrown up by the Regency. Classicism came in any number of forms from William Reid's plain Georgian house at Largs of 1811 (74), to Nash's sophisticated French-influenced Casina at Dulwich of 1797 (72), William Donthorn's aggressively geometrical design for a parsonage at Watlington of about 1824 (78), his delicate Italianate of the Moulton parsonage of 1831 (77), or Henry Bassett's austerely Italianate villa for Thomas Clarke of 1833 (73). Donthorn is a good example of the chameleon-like quality of Regency architects with their ability to design in any required style, although Gothic and Tudor dominate his later work (79). As the eclectic architect

Thomas Hopper declared: 'it is an architect's business to understand all styles, and to be prejudiced in favour of none'.

Perhaps the classic style for the Regency villa was the cottage orné, like that George Wightwick built for John Bedford near Penzance in 1833 (80). Although early examples can be found in the 1760s the style attained popularity around the turn of the century. With its rustic overtones it fitted in well with the Regency move to a simpler life, apparently more in tune with nature. The most famous cottage ornés, the Prince Regent's Royal Lodge at Windsor and the Duke of Bedford's Endsleigh, were built on the scale of a medium-sized country house; but these were exceptional. Most cottage ornés were

small, although much larger and better appointed than the cottages on which they were supposed to be modelled. Few lacked an adequate servants' wing.

By 1833 the idea of a cottage orné was falling swiftly out of fashion, but for A.W.N. Pugin such buildings were only proof of the degeneracy of contemporary architecture. The single hope in domestic as well as ecclesiastical architecture lay in a return to the Middle Ages, as he showed at St Marie's Grange, the house he built for himself near Salisbury in 1835 (81). It was a house that had no contemporary parallel, and was so novel that he had difficulty selling it a couple of years later.

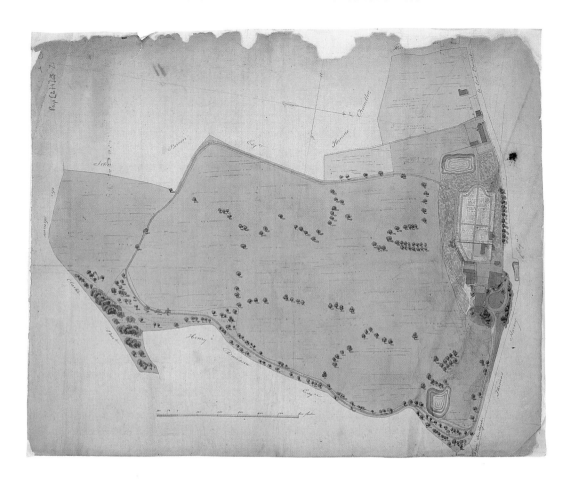

John Buonarotti Papworth
1775-1847
Design for Little Grove, Barnet,
London
62 Copy of an 1817 survey with
additions to the house blocked in,
1828
Pen and watercolour (515 × 640)

63 Plan showing the additions to the
house, new buildings and the
grounds landscaped, 1828
Pen and watercolour (510 × 650)

64 Plan of the approach to the house
with plan and elevation of the
proposed lodge, 1828
Pen and watercolour (455 × 630)

LITTLE Grove was typical of the substantial villas that surrounded London. It was bought in November 1827 by Frederick Cass for his youngest son Francis who immediately began to plan alterations. The architect was John Buonarotti Papworth, about 2,600 of whose drawings survive in the RIBA. Although Papworth never gained a major commission, he was a prolific architect, and the drawings, together with a biography written by his son and abstracts of his diaries, give an insight into the career of a second-rate London architect. His practice was all-encompassing; he could design anything from a handkerchief to a landscape park, and among his several books was *Hints on Ornamental Gardening* published in 1823.

As bought by Cass, Little Grove was a late eighteenth-century house of three storeys and seven bays set in fifty-four acres. Papworth first traced a survey plan of the surrounding land made in 1817 and then transferred that into a watercolour of the land as it was, but with the proposed additions to the house blocked in (62). This was pricked for transfer and a second drawing showing further alterations and a new farm, together with proposals for turning the farmland into a miniature park, was drawn to exactly the same scale (63). The surrounding farmland was to be carefully landscaped with surrounding shelter belts and clumps of trees. At the same time shrubberies and more extensive gardens were created near the house.

Little Grove was demolished in 1932 and the land built over.

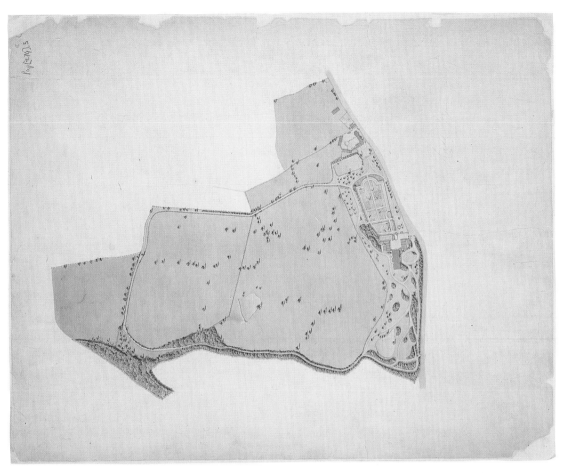

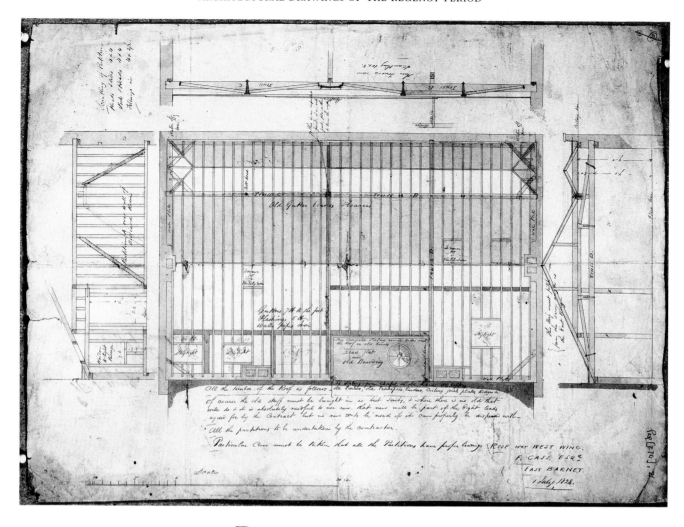

John Buonarotti Papworth
1775-1847
Design for Little Grove, Barnet,
London
65 Sections and plan of the details of
the scantlings of the roof over the
west wing, 1828
Pen and coloured washes
(470 × 645)

66 North elevation, 1828
Pen (445 × 620)

67 Ground plan, 1828
Pen and coloured washes
(460 × 640)

Papworth's plans for remodelling Little Grove can be compared with those Robert Adam made for Kenwood, being essentially cosmetic but with a certain amount of new building. Pilasters, formed of tiles fastened to the walls by hooks were to be added to the main facade, with a portico and a new wing to match that existing. The house was to be rendered, the main front in Atkinson's cement, the others in Roman cement, and all the window frames except those over the portico and in the basement were to be renewed.

Closely annotated with detailed information about the design, numbers 66 and 67 were part of the set of contract drawings made by Papworth and signed by Frederick Cass, the owner, and James Newman, the builder, in April 1828. Ten contract drawings survive: four plans, three sections (longitudinal and transverse with a further transverse section of the new wing), and three elevations, front and back and the side of the new wing. Number 65, however, is not a contract drawing but is a working drawing made on 1 July 1828, showing the roof structure of the new wing. Thus the details of the design were drawn up as the house progressed.

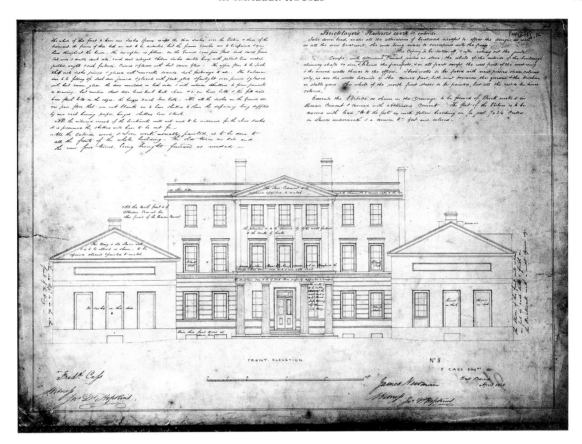

FRONT. ELEVATION.

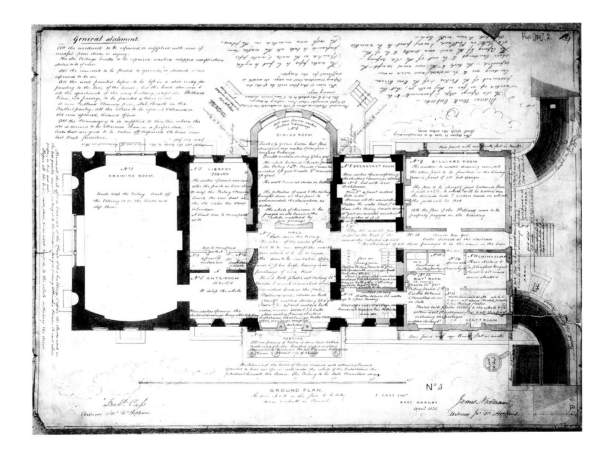

GROUND PLAN.

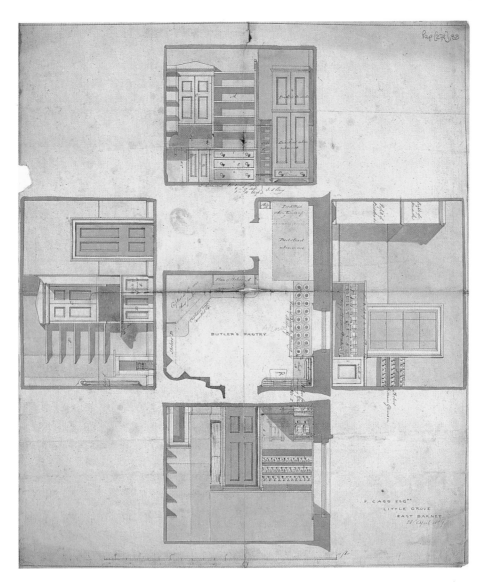

John Buonarotti Papworth
1775-1847
Design for Little Grove, Barnet,
London
68 Plan with elevations of four walls
laid out to show the fittings of the
butler's pantry, 1829
Pen and coloured washes
(625 × 525)

AMONG Papworth's most attractive and fascinating drawings are his
room schemes which show the new
room down to the last item. Exploded plans like these had been
common in the eighteenth century,
but they had been reserved for important rooms, principally to show
the plasterwork decoration. Papworth made such drawings for all the
significant new rooms, not only the
dining room and library, but also the
butler's pantry, the housekeeper's
room, the nursery, the servants' hall,
the housekeeper's store room, and
the china closet. Inscriptions on this
drawing refer to the shelves designed
to drain decanters and glasses, to a
trough which drained the water from
the decanters and to the butler's

hinged-bed which is shown both
down and up, when it disappeared
into a cupboard.

Concentration on fine rooms has
meant that little research has been
done into the functioning of such
office quarters. Papworth's plans
allow us to see how they worked,
what furniture they had, how it was
arranged, what decoration, if any,
they had on the walls. Clearly great
thought went into the design of these
rooms, although it is not clear how
exceptional Papworth was in making
such drawings.

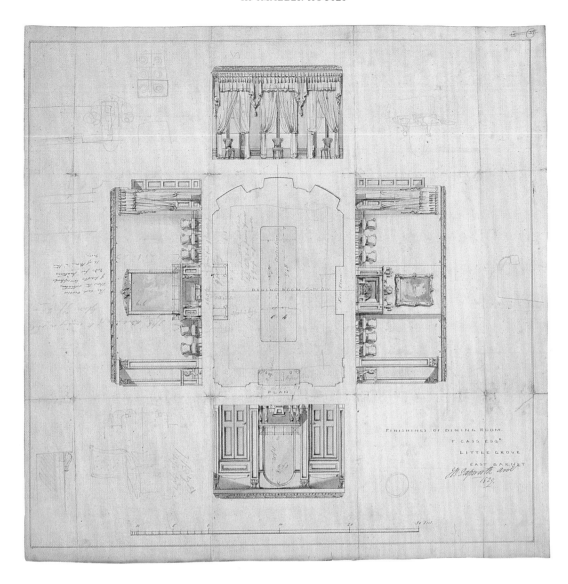

**John Buonarotti Papworth
1775-1847**
Design for Little Grove, Barnet,
London
69 Plan with elevations of four walls
laid out to show the finishings of the
dining room, 1829
Black and red pen with sepia and
blue washes (465 × 470)

Papworth's exploded plan shows the decoration of the dining room down to the last tassel, and its furnishing down to the last ornament on the mantelpiece. The contract drawings for Little Grove only dealt with the carcase of the house, further designs were made for fitting it up once work was underway. By the time this drawing was made in 1829 the architectural decoration of the dining room had already been decided (70-1). Its purpose was to show the proposed finishing of the room.

The curtains are particularly elaborate with a continuous pelmet running right across the curved window wall, with swags in between the windows and a run of tassels above. The drawing is a reminder that the restrained plasterwork of Regency rooms was supposed to be softened by the richness of the fabrics, particularly curtains. Few such rooms retain their fabrics and as a result they now have an undeserved air of gauntness.

Exploded plan drawings were effective in showing nearly every element of the room, except items standing away from the wall like the dining-room table.

John Buonarotti Papworth
1775-1847
Design for Little Grove, Barnet,
London
70 Plan and elevation of the end wall
of the dining room, 1828
Pen and wash (510 × 465)

Seventy-nine drawings survive for Little Grove, for every feature down to the smallest detail, many of them closely annotated so that there could be no confusion on the part of the workmen. The dining room was formed out of an existing room which was extended by throwing out a bow window. The first drawing, dated 14 June 1828, is for the windows, but a swift change of mind meant this was countermanded by another two days later ordering that French sashes be installed instead. By the end of the month drawings for the doors had been sent, and in September designs were being made for the architectural decoration of the walls. Four drawings survive for this, the first being for the cornice, dated 11 September 1828, the last, dated 7 November 1829, being for details of mouldings and enrichments.

Papworth gave the entrance wall a strong architectural feel, framing a central mirror (which is not shown in this drawing) between two pilasters, with doors on either side. Mirrors played an important part in the decoration of the room, with another, wider mirror set above the chimney-piece.

Annotations on the drawing show that much of the architectural detail had not been included in the contract and was to be charged as extra.

John Buonarotti Papworth
1775-1847
Design for Little Grove, Barnet,
London
71 Front and side elevation of the
capital for the dining room pilasters,
1829
Sepia and red pen with sepia, blue
and yellow washes (525 × 650)

Two full-size drawings survive
for the capitals of the pilasters in the
dining room: one the original sketch
design and this, the working drawing
made from it, pricked for transfer.
Full-scale working drawings are the
least likely part of any related group
of drawings to survive, but for an
elaborate capital like this they were
necessary if the architect was to be
certain that his decorative intentions
would be followed. While elevations,
plans and perspectives were often
preserved for their intrinsic merit
this was seldom true of such large-
scale working drawings. One of the
values of the Papworth collection is
that it represents all aspects of
architectural drawing.

The orders remained central to
architecture, and the first task of any
trainee architect was to master the art
of drawing them. This is an interesting Greek variant of a Corinthian
capital. The drawing is evidence of
the high quality of Regency
draughtsmanship, something with
which Papworth was particularly
concerned. He was appointed the
first director of the Government
School of Design which opened in
May 1837, but was forced to retire
after fifteen months when the government cut the school's grant.

John Nash 1752-1835
Record drawing attributed to George
Stanley Repton 1786-1858 of the
Casina, Dulwich, Southwark,
London
72 Ground floor plan, elevation of
south front, details of cornice, plinth
and junction between full-length
window and plinth *c.* 1797-8
Pen (405 × 335)

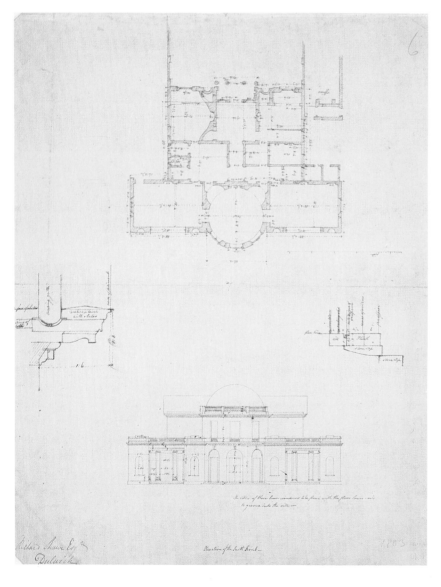

Bankruptcy was always a threat to Regency architects, particularly those still trying to establish themselves. John Nash moved to Wales when his attempt to set himself up as an architect and speculative builder in London failed in 1783. He returned thirteen years later and soon established himself as one of the capital's leading architects, reshaping much of central London.

The Casina at Dulwich was designed for Richard Shawe who had made his fortune the year before as solicitor to Warren Hastings during his trial. It was one of the houses that re-established Nash in London, and was exhibited at the Royal Academy in 1797, the first year that he appeared there. It is a fine example of his French-inspired neoclassicism, an example of a style popular in the 1780s and 90s among advanced architects like Holland, for whom Nash had worked.

As the paper for this drawing is watermarked 1803 this must be a copy drawing and may be by G.S. Repton with whose copy notebook it should be compared (58). The drawing marks the brief alliance between Nash and Humphry Repton, who laid out the grounds of the Casina.

The Casina was demolished in 1906 and its site is now a housing estate.

Henry Bassett 1803-c. 1850
Design for the Eagles, West Hill,
Highgate, London
73 Perspective, 1833
Watercolour (335 × 510)

Bassett never fulfilled the early promise which saw him awarded gold medals, first by the Society of Arts when he was twenty and then by the Royal Academy two years later. Apart from this villa in Highgate for Thomas Clarke, only one country house and a couple of villas in Regent's Park are known to have been designed by him. Instead he made his career as a surveyor, being employed on the Southampton estate in Bloomsbury which he gave as his address when exhibiting at the Royal Academy. As well as property in Bloomsbury Lord Southampton owned land to the east of Regent's Park, and in Highgate around Fitzroy House.

Fitzroy House was demolished in 1826 and an attempt was made to develop an estate of substantial detached houses. Building leases were sold from 1832, including one for Beechwood which was probably designed by George Basevi. The development was not a success and when the estate was sold in 1840 most of the plots were empty. The Eagles, now 33 West Hill, was at the southern end of the estate and now houses the Soviet trade delegation.

This watercolour shows what must have attracted the judges in his youth, for it is a highly accomplished work. The Italianate style became popular in the 1820s and 30s, and in an increasingly debased form became the common vocabulary of the London builder.

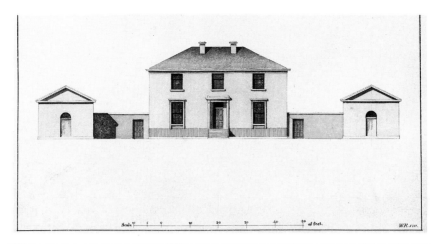

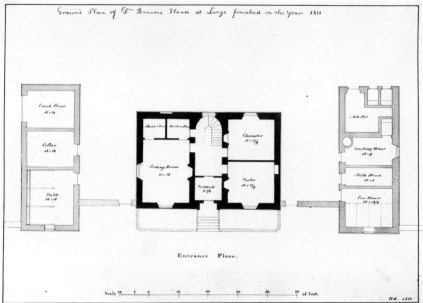

William Reid *fl.* **1795-1833**
Design for a house at Largs,
Strathclyde
74 Elevation, 1811
Sepia pen and wash (240 × 295)

75 Ground plan, 1811
Sepia pen and wash (220 × 285)

Reid's design for Dr Brown shows how a simple astylar Georgian style marked by symmetry and lack of ornament survived well into the nineteenth century, particularly among relatively humble buildings like farmhouses or rectories. Reid was a minor architect living in Glasgow whose practice extended as far south as Carlisle. His chief works were in Paisley, near Glasgow, where he designed St George's Church and the County Buildings.

His connection with Cumbria probably arose through Peter Nicholson, another Glasgow architect who was surveyor to the County of Cumberland in 1808-10 and moved to London in 1810. Designs for Castletown, Cumbria, dated 1811, are signed *Reid and Nicholson Architects*. Reid also made unexecuted designs dated 1822 for a gaol in Carlisle.

Presumably Reid's partnership with Nicholson did not survive the latter's removal to London.

Dr Brown's house can almost certainly be identified with Broomfield House which was demolished in 1963. This was one of the marine villas round Castle Bay, Largs, known locally as The Crescent. Apart from the small vestibule and curved staircase the ground floor had only three rooms, a parlour, a bedroom, and an eating room with a closet and butler's pantry, the latter no more than a closet itself. The gentility of a stable and coach house was matched by a cow house and dairy in the other wing.

James Hakewill 1778-1843
Design for a villa
76 Plan and elevation, 1829
Pen, pink wash and watercolour
(515 × 355)

G.W. AYLMER was somewhat surprised when he received this drawing, together with a first-floor plan and two alternative plans. He had not even decided that he wanted to build a house and had only mentioned it casually to Hakewill. Hakewill tried to persuade him to take the first site on the Calverley estate at Tunbridge Wells in Kent, where Decimus Burton was laying out a park of detached villas in shared grounds. Aylmer liked the plan but not the elevation. The layout owes much to Soane's villas, particularly in the narrow cross-vaulted entrance passage, and may show the influence of Pell Wall House, Shropshire which Soane illustrated in *Designs for Public and Private Buildings* of 1828. Aylmer did not care for the disturbance which building the other villas on the Calverley estate would cause, and wrote to Hakewill saying that he did not intend to build, although he did offer to pay for the cost of the drawings.

Hakewill was better known as an architectural writer than as an architect. His books range from *A Picturesque Tour in the Island of Jamaica* of 1825, to *Plans, Sections, and Elevations of the Abattoirs of Paris, with Considerations of Their Adoption in London* of 1828, and *An Attempt to Determine the Exact Character of Elizabethan Architecture* of 1835. Only a handful of buildings are known to have been designed by him and it is not clear why G.W. Aylmer went to him when considering building a house.

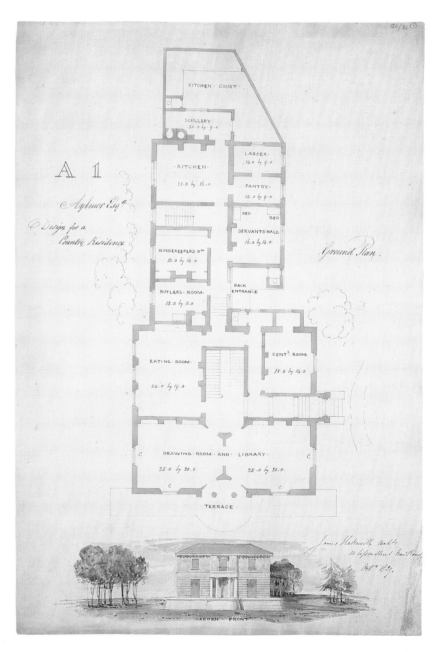

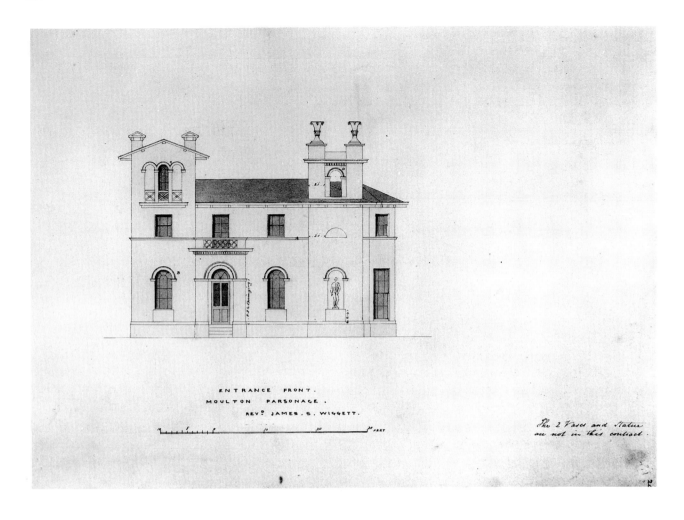

ENTRANCE FRONT.
MOULTON PARSONAGE.
REV? JAMES. S. WIGGETT.

The 2 Vases and Statue are not in this contract.

William John Donthorn 1799-1859
Record drawing of the parsonage at
Moulton, Norfolk
77 Elevation, 1831
Pen and coloured washes
(305 × 490)

Record drawing of a design for a
parsonage at Watlington, Norfolk
78 Elevation, *c.* 1824
Pen and sepia wash (335 × 485)

Record drawing of the parsonage at
Trunch, Norfolk
79 Elevation, 1832
Pen and sepia wash (225 × 310)

L̲ARGE numbers of vicarages were erected during the first decades of the nineteenth century, and they proved a useful source of work for many minor or provincial architects. Joseph Langwith of Grantham built a series in Lincolnshire and Leicestershire, George Wightwick of Plymouth designed ten in Cornwall; but William Donthorn built nearly twenty, mainly in Norfolk. They were such an important part of his career that he devoted one of the four volumes of his architectural drawings now in the RIBA to them.

The design for Watlington for the Rev. E. Cobbold was never executed.

Donthorn developed an antiquarian interest as a boy and exhibited architectural views at the Norwich Society of Artists from the age of sixteen. From this he progressed to become a pupil of Wyatville, and shared with him the ability to design in whatever style was required. Moulton Parsonage is in the Italianate style. Watlington is a severely geometrical example of neoclassicism, Trunch is Tudor. Donthorn's most original work is his stripped neoclassicism which seems to look back to such French neoclassicists as Boullée and Ledoux. Like Smirke and Soane he was seeking a new style in which the classical orders became almost irrelevant, but his gauntness can have appealed to few, and his later work is dominated by Tudor designs.

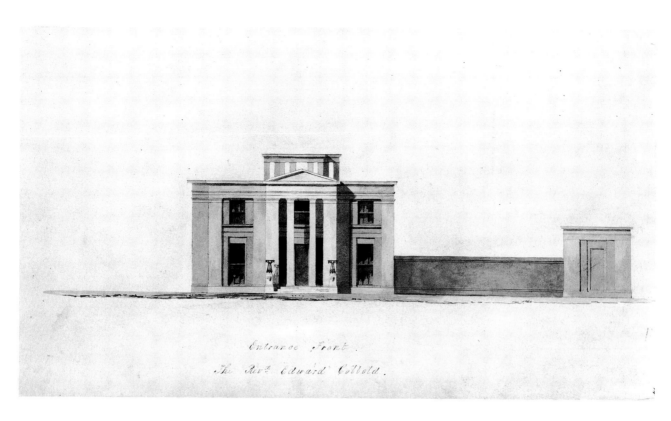

Entrance Front.
The Revd. Edward Cobbold.

Entrance Elevation
TRUNCH. REVD THOMAS TYRTON

George Wightwick 1802-1872
Record drawing of a cottage orné
near Penzance, Cornwall, for John
Bedford
80 Plans and elevations of the
ground and first floor, 1833-4
Pen and watercolour (415 × 315)

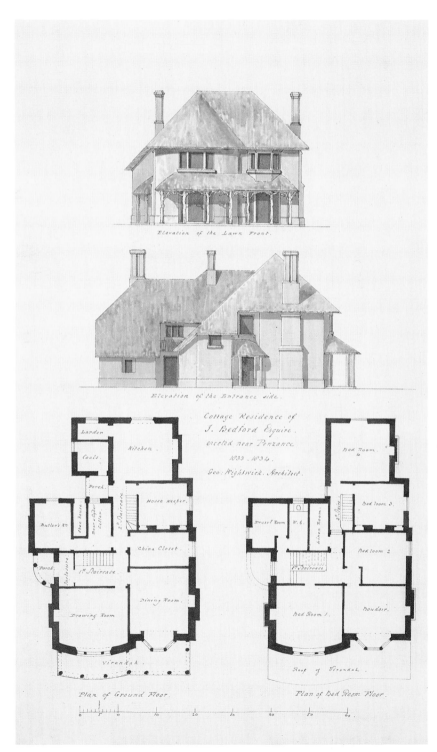

No type of building epitomises the Regency better than the cottage orné, a house built on the scale of a villa but in the style of a cottage. Behind it lay the desire for the picturesque, a desire which saw enchantment in the country cottage, not as it was but as portrayed by Gainsborough. The vogue for lodges and estate workers' houses built in a thatched and half-timbered mock vernacular was a related phenomenon, but whereas such cottages were seldom designed for practicality, a cottage orné was well appointed with servants' quarters. A perspective for John Bedford's cottage orné also survives but was not copied into the record volume which comprised only plans, elevations and sections.

Typically, Bedford's cottage orné was built by the sea. Steephill, Hans Stanley's house on the Isle of Wight built about 1764 and probably the first true cottage orné, had a remote coastal setting and during the first decades of the nineteenth century many seaside resorts were dotted with cottage ornés. The affectation of rustic life appealed to all levels of polite society, from the Prince Regent and the Duke of Bedford down, but the aristocracy and gentry never built cottage ornés as their seats, using them merely as escapes. For many of the middle classes — retired professional men, widows and younger sons of the gentry — a cottage orné was their only home.

Augustus Welby Northmore Pugin
1812-1852
Topographical view of St Marie's
Grange, Wiltshire
81 Perspective, *c.* 1835-7
Watercolour (125 × 175)

PUGIN killed Regency architecture, replacing its stylistic ambiguities with his own dogmatic idealism, first revealed in his *Contrasts* in 1836. This claimed that only Gothic architecture was morally acceptable. Pugin had developed his knowledge working for his father, who published a series of books illustrated with examples of medieval architecture, but allied to it a theory of design alien to Regency thinking.

St Marie's Grange was Pugin's first building, designed for himself, and presenting a radically different vision of Gothic domestic architecture to anything that had gone before. As Pugin wrote, it was 'the only modern building that is compleat in every part in the antient style'. His diary shows that masonry work began on 26 January 1835, although the contract was only signed and sealed on the 29th. He first drew at St Marie's Grange on 11 September, and he began sleeping there on the 15th of that month. Unfortunately, he had only been in the house for just over a year when his wife's ill-health and the arrival of another child forced him to move out. The house remained empty until 1841 when it was sold, possibly after some alterations by Pugin.

IV CHURCHES

THE very first years of the Regency saw the erection of a number of interesting and innovative churches: George Steuart's St Chad's, Shrewsbury, of 1790-2, S.P. Cockerell's St Mary's, Banbury, of 1792-7, Thomas Telford's St Michael's, Madeley, of 1794-6. But sadly, the RIBA lacks any drawings for them. They were isolated works, and the flame of church building was snuffed out during the Napoleonic Wars when fewer churches were built than at any other time since the Commonwealth. But this period of despondency was soon to be replaced by the most vigorous age of church building since the Reformation, an age only eclipsed by the extraordinary ecclesiastical fervour of the Victorians. It was an age when an impressive number of new churches were built but the result was so vilified by the next generation that even today they find few defenders.

The years immediately before Waterloo brought the first intimations of a new interest in church building. Thomas Hardwick's St Marylebone, London, of 1813, Thomas Rickman's and John Cragg's St George's, Everton, Liverpool, of 1812, and Joseph Gwilt's St Margaret's, Lee, (100) of 1813 were all signs of a growing realisation that the stock of churches was inadequate and had to be improved both in number and in size. The rising popularity of the Methodists made the church authorities realise that they had to act if they were not to become totally irrelevant in the cities which were

swelling daily under the impact of the industrial revolution. The result was the passing of the Church Building Act of 1818 which allowed new parishes to be created by dividing old ones and new churches built in parishes containing not less than four thousand people. Churches could also be built in parishes where there was seating for less than a thousand parishioners or where more than a thousand people lived more than four miles from the parish church. To finance this the Commissioners were given £1 million to disburse in grants.

Unlike the Fifty New Churches of a century earlier the emphasis was not on architectural display but on size and economy. The aim was to get as many people into church as possible and at the most economical rate. The Commissioners' success was considerable. They built 214 churches at an average cost per head of £8.

With the emphasis on economy the ingenious churches of the 1790s proved of little value as models. Their very innovation and novel shapes meant they were too expensive. The problem faced was very similar to that Wren had analysed in a memorandum to the Fifty New Churches Commissioners: what was the maximum number of people that could be fitted into a church and still be able to hear the vicar preaching? The Anglican liturgy was based on the primacy of the word, the lessons and the sermon, and it was not enough just to see the sacrament of

communion. The solution the Commissioners came up with was much the same as that put forward by Wren. This was not surprising as Soane, one of the three attached architects to the Office of Works who were asked to put forward sample plans, spent several days with his pupils surveying St James's, Piccadilly, the church where Wren encapsulated his ideals most clearly.

The answer was a rectangular church with little or no chancel, galleries to fit in as many people as possible, and a tall tower at the west end to make the church stand out. St John the Baptist, Hoxton, (85-96) is a typical early Commissioners' church, and was designed by Francis Edwards who worked for a time in Soane's office. Architectural elaboration is kept to a minimum, except in the west end and the tower. Nevertheless, it is a handsome building. Later the Commissioners were to discover that they could build churches more cheaply, and churches built from the late 1820s are less impressive.

Inside St John's were two levels of galleries and an extra set of benches in the central aisle to increase the number of free seats. Free seats were one of the key aims of the Commissioners. A balance had to be struck between the income that could be derived from letting pews, a standard practice at the time, and the need to encourage the lower orders to come to church. At Hoxton there were 813 paying pew-holders bringing in £590 18s a year, and 829 free seats. Inevitably these free seats were at the back of the church.

St John's was built to a classical design, like nearly all the early London churches. In the provinces Gothic prevailed, generally because it was thought to be cheaper. Many examples of Commissioners' Gothic are thin, owing their detail largely to eighteenth-century Gothic models but without their lightness of touch. There was no attempt to emulate Gothic building techniques and no understanding of medieval architecture as an evolving style. But the Regency was a time of great interest in the buildings of the Middle Ages, and a stream of publications by John Britton, A.C. Pugin and Thomas Rickman soon provided architects with a mass of accurate medieval architectural details. Of these three Rickman was the most interesting as he became one of the Regency's most prolific ecclesiastical architects. He understood the structure of a medieval church and could reproduce its detail convincingly. When given the resources he was able to look beyond the limitations of Commissioners' Gothic and design a church that came significantly nearer to the medieval original. St John's, Oulton, in Yorkshire (97-9), where he was working for a private client, is one of his most successful works. This, with its chancel and focus on the high altar was far removed from Gwilt's church at Lee where the pulpit blocks the view of the altar. Nevertheless, Edward Lapidge's small chapel at Doddington in Cheshire (104) is typical of the sort of Gothic church still being designed in 1836.

The publication in 1836 of *Contrasts; or A Parallel Between the Noble Edifices of the Fourteenth and Fifteenth Centuries, and similar Buildings of the Present Day* by A.W.N. Pugin revolutionised attitudes towards church design. With devastating polemic Pugin attacked the Commissioners' pragmatic approach to providing the maximum number of seats for the money they had been allocated. Such churches did not comply with what he saw as the demands of the 'true' Catholic church, whose buildings had to be designed accurately on medieval models. Some architects resisted like George Wightwick, but they had little success, and in 1837 the future belonged to Pugin.

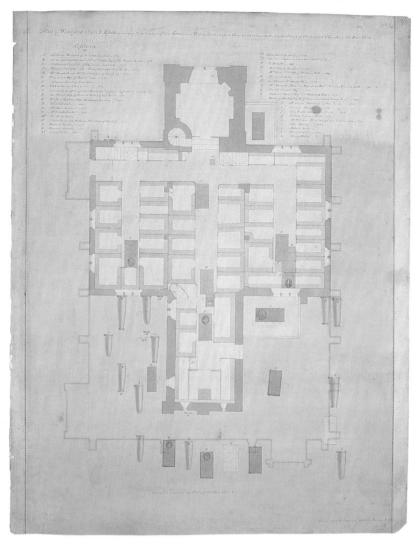

Charles Bacon c. 1784-1818
Survey plan of the Church and
graveyard of St Mary the Virgin,
Woodford, Redbridge, London
82 Plan, 1816
Pen and coloured washes
(635 × 500)

Bacon made this survey showing
the position of the tombs and graves
before they were removed for the
rebuilding of the church under his
direction. The grey rectangles represent the memorial slabs, the raised
mounds the site of the graves. The
red line indicates the extent of the
proposed new church. St Mary the
Virgin had long been too small and
by 1811 the fabric was also ruinous.
Bacon took down the side walls of
the chancel and extended the aisles
the length of the chancel. At the
same time the walls were raised, the
north and south windows enlarged
and galleries installed.

In 1816 Charles Bacon's career
looked well established with a series
of official posts to his name and the
beginning of a promising private
career. Trained in the Office of
Works, he had shared first prize in
1809 with G.S. and J.A. Repton in a
competition for the design of public
buildings in Westminster. These
were never erected, but in 1811 he
succeeded his former master, J.T.
Groves, as clerk of the works at
Whitehall, Westminster and St
James's. To this he added responsibility for the Royal Mews at Charing
Cross in 1815, together with the post
of architect to Ely Cathedral and
surveyor for the county of Middlesex
in 1816. In the same year he was also
appointed architect to Princess Charlotte. Two years later he died, aged
only thirty-four.

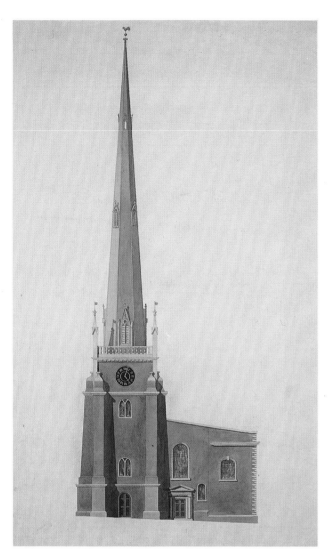

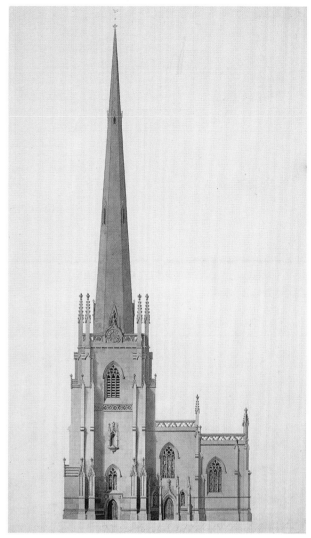

Thomas Rickman 1776-1841
Survey drawings of the Church of
St Martin, Birmingham
83 Elevation of the west end, 1820
Pen and wash with some gold
(645 × 440)

84 Elevation of the west end
showing the facade recased in stone
and the whole re-Gothicised in
Decorated style, 1820
Pen and watercolour (630 × 430)

Sᴛ ᴍᴀʀᴛɪɴ's was Birmingham's
mother church. It had been recased
in brick in about 1690, apart from the
spire which was partly rebuilt by
John Chesshire in 1781. Rickman
planned to restore the church to what
he considered its original medieval
appearance. Nothing came of Rickman's scheme, and in 1853-5 P.C.
Hardwick restored St Martin's, only
for it to be demolished and replaced
(except for the tower) in 1873-5. It
was later bombed in the Second
World War.

1820 was a suitable year for Rickman to seek a Birmingham commis-

sion, as he had opened an office there
under his pupil Henry Hutchinson. It
was Rickman who created the basic
divisions by which we still distinguish
medieval architecture when he published *An Attempt to Discriminate the
Styles of English Architecture from the
Conquest to the Reformation* in 1817.
The prestige this brought him meant
that though he came late to
architecture, only setting up an office
in Liverpool in 1817 when he was over
forty, he had established himself as a
leading church architect by 1820. By
the time of his death in 1841 he had
built or altered over sixty churches.

Francis Edwards 1784-1857
Contract drawings for the Church of
St John the Baptist, Hoxton,
Hackney, London
85 Elevation of the west front, 1824
Pen and coloured washes
(450 × 685)

86 Elevation of the south front, 1824
Pen and coloured washes
(450 × 685)

87 Elevation of the north front, 1824
Pen and coloured washes
(450 × 685)

Hoxton had been a hamlet with-

in a parish of St Leonard Shoreditch, but by 1801 the population of the parish had risen to thirty-five thousand, and a decade later it stood at forty-four thousand with only the single church to serve it. It was to deal with such situations that the 'Million Pound Act' had been passed in 1818, providing a fund to finance new churches.

The 1½ acre site of St John's, Hoxton, was bought for 1,000 gns and designs were agreed in 1824. The church was consecrated on 26 June 1828, the total cost, including the graveyard, being £16,444.

Francis Edwards entered Soane's office in 1806 as an 'improver'. After leaving it in 1810 he worked four days a week in the office of another

former pupil of Soane's, Henry Seward, who had left Soane's office in 1808 after a number of years as a clerk. Seward was the initial choice of architect for St John's, but on being appointed Assistant Surveyor-General in 1823 he gave up private practice and resigned his post. Edwards took his place, the commission allowing him to establish an independent practice, although this is his only recorded church. An unforeseen benefit resulted, from the establishment of the Imperial Gas Works Company in Hoxton in 1823 which appointed him their surveyor, presumably on the strength of his position as church architect.

The influence of Soane is particularly strong in the west front.

Proposed New Church

Elevation of the South Front.

New Church

Elevation of the North Front.

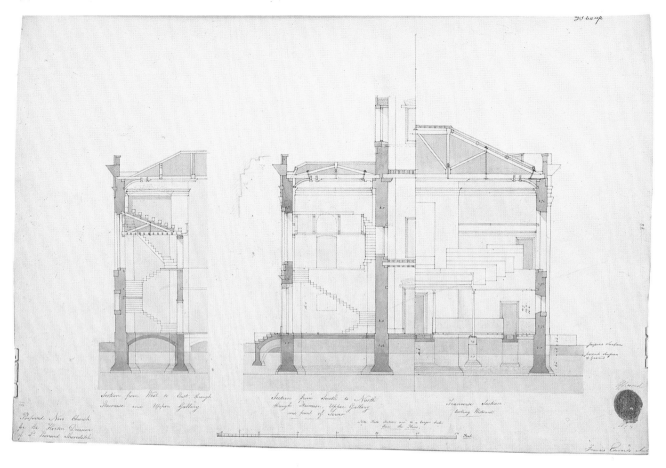

Francis Edwards 1784-1857
Contract drawings for the Church of
St John the Baptist, Hoxton, Hackney, London

88 Sections from west to east
through the staircase and upper
gallery, from south to north through
the staircase, upper gallery and part
of the tower, and transverse section
looking westwards, 1824
Pen and coloured washes
(450 × 685)

89 Longitudinal section, 1824
Pen and coloured washes
(450 × 685)

90 Transverse section, 1824
Pen and coloured washes
(450 × 685)

A COMPLETE set of fifty-six contract drawings bound in a single
volume survives for St John's. All are
signed by Francis Edwards, bear the
seal of the Church Commissioners
and the stamp 'Approved 1824'.
Some are also signed by the various
contractors, but many signatures and
dates have been trimmed to fit the
volume. The drawings allow the construction of the church to be followed
in minute detail, down to the last
element of the woodwork. By contrast in the seventeenth century
much of the detail of decoration in
Wren's City churches had been left
to the individual craftsmen.
Although damaged in the war and
altered, particularly in 1902 when the
ceiling and walls were decorated by
J.A. Reeve with scenes from the
Revelation of St John, Edwards's interior remains essentially intact.

Edwards's drawings show how the
convention on colour coding in
architectural drawings had become
widely accepted. Each different
structural element has its own colour,
blue for stone and glass, pink for
brick, grey for iron, light yellow for
structural timbers, light brown for
joiners' work and deep yellow for
floor boards. There is no key, and
only on the facades is 'stone' or 'brick'
written in.

Longitudinal Section

Proposed New Church
for the Horton Division

Transverse Section

Proposed New Church
for the Horton Division
of St Leonard Shoreditch

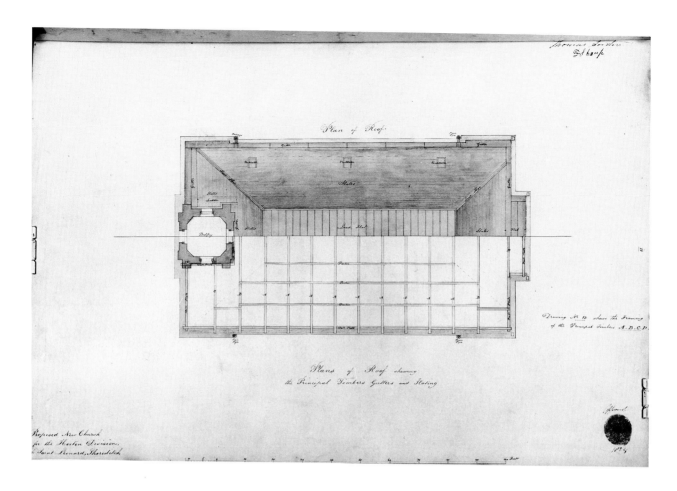

Francis Edwards 1784-1857
Contract drawings for the Church of
St John the Baptist, Hoxton,
Hackney, London
91 Plan of the roof and roof timbers,
1824
Pen and coloured washes
(450 × 685)

92 Ground plan, 1824
Pen and coloured washes
(450 × 685)

93 Gallery plan, 1824
Pen and coloured washes
(450 × 685)

THE Commissioners' churches were designed to make as many seats available for worshippers as was possible, in the most economical way. Thus Edwards's aim was to design a church where as many people as possible could hear and see the service. The result lay firmly in the tradition of the Protestant preaching box perfected by Wren at St James's, Piccadilly, in 1676, a rectangular body with galleries, and with the altar at the east end only slightly set back from the body of the church.

According to the tables on the ground and gallery plans the church could hold 1,988 people, 813 in the nave, 829 in the gallery and 276 charity children in the upper gallery. Equally important was the rent that the pews brought in as this was to be an important part of the parish's income. The best-placed pews were valued at £1 per annum for seven seats, the worst, for five people, were 6s. In all there were to be 813 paying pew-holders, bringing in an income of £590 18s a year, with 829 seats at the rear and side of the church and in the aisle which were free.

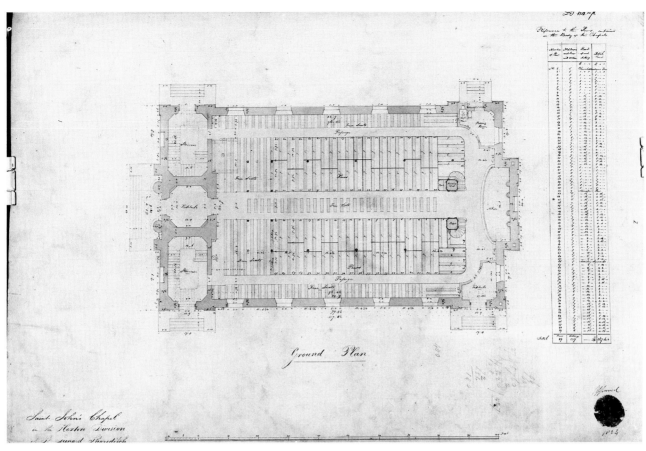

Ground Plan

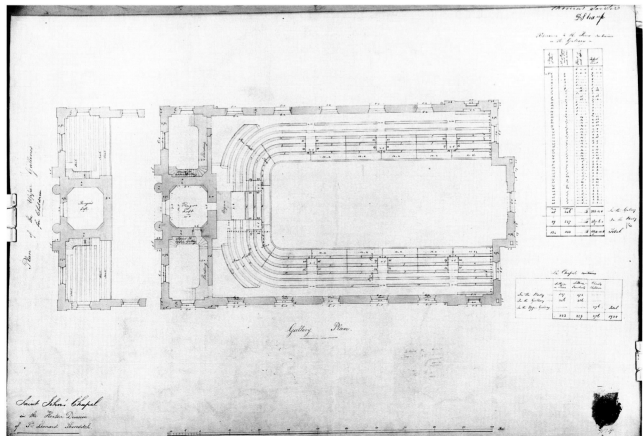

Gallery Plan

Francis Edwards 1784-1857
Contract drawings for the Church of
St John the Baptist, Hoxton, Hackney, London

94 Elevation, section, and part-plan
of the cupola and profiles of
mouldings, 1824
Pen and coloured washes
(450 × 685)

95 Details of the timber structure of the
roof, 1824
Pen and coloured washes (450 × 685)

96 Details of ironwork, 1824
Pen and coloured washes (450 × 685)

THE fifty-six drawings by Francis Edwards for St John the Baptist, Hoxton, cover every last detail of the church's design. For the Commissioners this was the best way of ensuring that the costs of each church did not overrun. By contrast Henry Flitcroft's 1731 designs for St Giles-in-the-Fields, London, show only the basic plan, elevations and sections. The result is that we can establish far more precisely the exact structural techniques used in building St John's.

Iron had been used to strengthen timber roof structures during the second half of the eighteenth century, but this increased significantly between 1780 and 1850, which was the heyday of cast-iron in building. At Hoxton Edwards only used iron to reinforce joints or for short pillars, but by 1824 it was possible to use cast-iron beams that were longer than even the largest timber girders. Nash used extensive quantities of cast-iron beams at Buckingham House between 1826 and 1828, and by 1840 they were well established, although by then cast-iron was beginning to be replaced by wrought-iron.

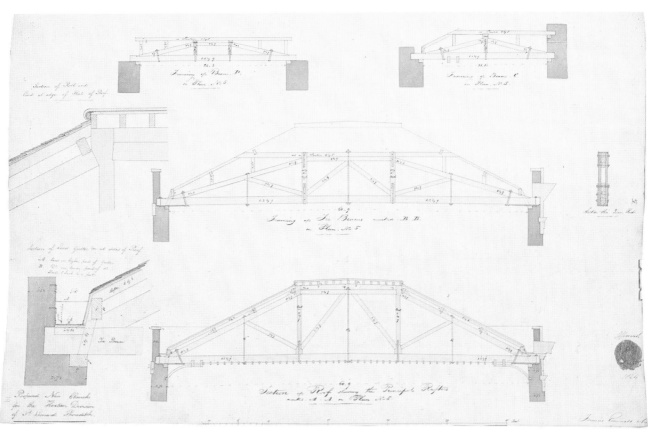

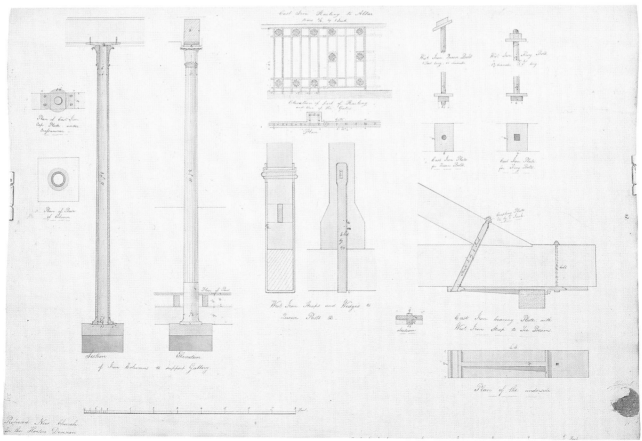

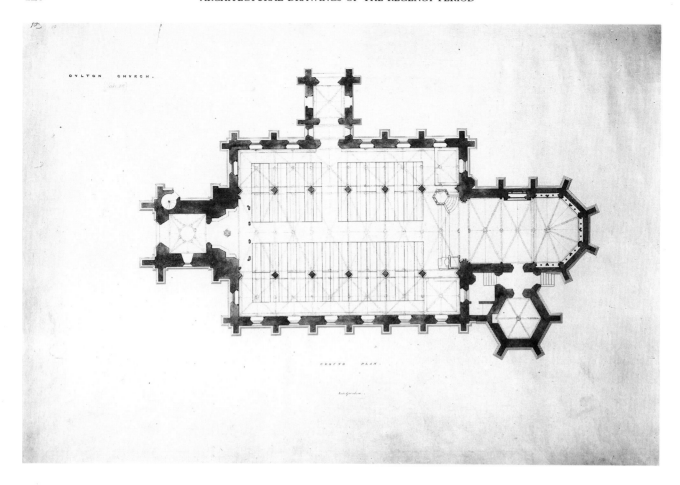

Thomas Rickman 1776-1841
Design drawn by Henry Hutchinson
1800-1831 for the Church of St John,
Oulton, West Yorkshire
97 Plan, 1827-9
Black and blue pen with sepia
wash (660 × 995)

98 South elevation, 1827-9
Pen (660 × 995)

99 Longitudinal section, 1827-9
Pen and blue wash (660 × 995)

Rickman's diaries make it possible to follow the progress of the
Oulton commission. On 6 January
1827 he received a letter from John
Blayds junior of Oulton, near Leeds,
announcing that his father intended
building a church which they wanted
Rickman to design. Four days later
he was in Leeds. He approved the
site, digging a trial hole to test the
foundations, and made sketches of a
possible plan and elevation. These
were shown to the elder Blayds who
ordered that they should be drawn
up immediately and accepted Rickman's rough estimate of £7,500.

After two further days' sketching
in the office Rickman left the plans
to be drawn up while he visited
Cheltenham. On the 27th he notes
that Henry Hutchinson had finished
all the drawings for Oulton which
looked very well, and after a couple
of days' designing stained glass, the
completed drawings were sent off on
2 February.

On 14 February the Blaydses
wrote approving the scheme, subject
only to a small alteration. Finally, on
3 March Rickman was at Oulton
again, where the alteration was soon
agreed and the go-ahead was given,
two months after Rickman had first
been approached. The result was one
of Rickman's most successful churches, its medieval form, with a
marked chancel, a distinct change
from the Georgian tradition main-
tained by the Commissioners'
churches.

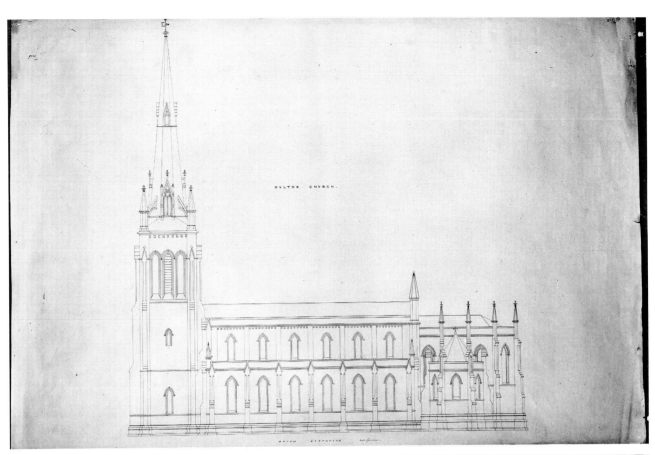

OVLTON CHVRCH.

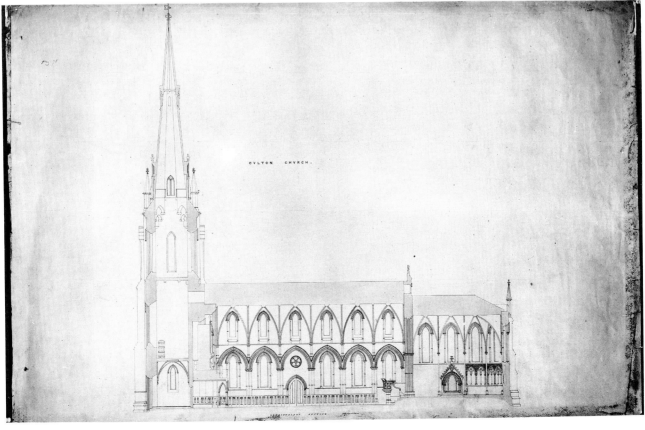

OVLTON CHVRCH.

Joseph Gwilt 1784-1863
Design for the Church of
St Margaret,
Lee, Lewisham, London
100 Interior perspective, 1813
Pen and watercolour
(275 × 185)

INTERIOR OF LEE CHURCH JOS. GWILT ARCH.T
BUILT A.D. 1814
ALLUDED TO AT PAGES 23 &25

T HE old church at Lewisham was demolished in 1813 to make way for a new building, although the tower was kept. Gwilt had already built a cottage for Thomas Brandrom, one of the churchwardens, and presumably owed the commission to him. The foundation stone was laid on 15 September 1813 and the building cost £4,200. This was partly raised on subscriptions, partly borrowed at interest. By 1841 St Margaret's was too small and was demolished. Although it predates the 1818 Million Pound Act, St Margaret's is typical of the thin Gothic churches that were built in great numbers under the act, with galleries and a reading desk in the centre hiding the altar, for Anglican worship was still dominated by the primacy of the word.

Gwilt is best known as a writer on architectural and antiquarian topics, and in particular for his new edition of Sir William Chambers's *Treatise on the Decorative Part of Civil Architecture* published in 1825. He held a succession of surveying positions, to the Commissioners of Sewers for Surrey, to the Grocers' and Waxchandlers' Companies and to the Imperial Fire Assurance Company, and much of his practice came from consultations with the Office of Woods and Forests and other official bodies. His volume of work is relatively small, but he was an elegant draughtsman.

George Stanley Repton 1786-1858
Design for the Chapel of St Philip,
Regent Street, Westminster, London
101 Interior perspective, 1819
Watercolour (245 × 460)

ST PHILIP'S was designed as a parochial chapel within the parish of St James's, Piccadilly. The moving force behind its erection was the Rev. Edward Repton, and the architect was his brother George Stanley Repton. It was set at the lower end of the new Regent Street. The foundation stone was laid in May 1819 and the church was consecrated in April 1820.

Charles Cockerell recorded in his diary in 1822 that Mr Reid, the builder, had told him that the original contract had been for £12,000, but that so many changes were made that his final bill included £3,000 for extras. The scagliola columns alone cost £500, although they were done in the cheapest manner, while the bill for glazing and painting came to more than £1,100.

Drawings in J. Britton's *Illustrations of Public Buildings* (1825) show that this is a preliminary design, with the chapel as built varying significantly. The number and layout of piers differ, an extra gallery was installed supported by the columns and a skylight was placed in the centre of the ceiling as the constricted site limited the light from the windows. However, the arrangement of the pulpit and reading desk on either side of the altar, restricting the view as little as possible — on which J.B. Papworth commented in *Illustrations* — was kept.

The church was demolished early this century.

Ignatius Bonomi c. 1787-1870
Survey drawing of Durham
Cathedral, Durham
102 Elevation of the end of the south
transept, 1835
Pen and wash (750 × 620)

IGNATIUS Bonomi was the son of
Joseph Bonomi (53), an Italian who
had come to England to work as a
draughtsman for Robert Adam before setting up an independent practice in 1784. He trained in his father's
office, but on Joseph's death in 1808
Ignatius, then twenty-one, was left
responsible for his mother and his
brothers and sisters.

Bonomi tried to use his father's
contacts, particularly with James
Wyatt who had been a close friend,
to find a job in London, perhaps in
the Office of Works. When that
failed he took advantage of the one
substantial commission left by his
father to establish himself as a provincial architect, where competition
was less strong even if demand
needed to be created. His father had
prepared a scheme for remodelling
Skelton Castle near Guisborough in
Yorkshire in 1805, but it was only in
1809 that work began. Emboldened
by this Ignatius established himself
in Durham where he acquired the
post of County Surveyor in 1813,
taking over the building of the County Gaol and Assize Court, a substantial commission that had run into
difficulties.

As the only professional architect — apart from John Dobson in
Newcastle — between Edinburgh
and York, Bonomi soon created a
substantial practice covering County
Durham and the north part of Yorkshire.

Ignatius Bonomi *c.* **1787-1870**
Design for Durham Cathedral,
Durham
103 Elevation, section and part-plan
of the end of the south transept
showing proposed restoration, 1836
Pen and wash (750 × 620)

Durham Cathedral had been a
centre of controversy in 1797-1805
when James Wyatt had not only
repaired the east end but proposed
rearranging the choir, demolishing
the galilee and building a new central
spire. Successful opposition by the
Society of Antiquaries in 1798 prevented this, but in 1801-2 the old
medieval revestry south of the choir
was removed, the aim apparently
being to purify the Norman cathedral
of all later accretions. This also
seems to have been the intention of
Ignatius Bonomi and his mason Thomas Jackson, who began restoring
the south front in 1827. A conscious
effort was made to reproduce the
original mouldings and capitals.

These two drawings show a more
drastic attempt to purify the Norman
cathedral, suggesting replacing the
six-light perpendicular window with
a very large Norman one, whose
traces could still be distinguished.
This was not carried out.

Bonomi's proposed restoration
made every effort to be accurate,
showing how far the understanding
of medieval architecture had progressed since Wyatt's day, thanks to the
work of men like Rickman. In the
rigour of his scheme Bonomi anticipates the thoroughgoing restorations
carried out by the Victorians, where
evidence of different periods of
building work were swept away in
favour of a single unified church.

These drawings were presented by
Bonomi to the Institute of British
Architects in July 1836, together with
a letter containing a description of
the restoration.

Edward Lapidge 1779-1860
Design for a chapel at Doddington,
Cheshire
104 Plan of the ground floor, part-
elevation of the south and west
fronts and parts of transverse
section, 1836
Pen and pencil (600 × 480)

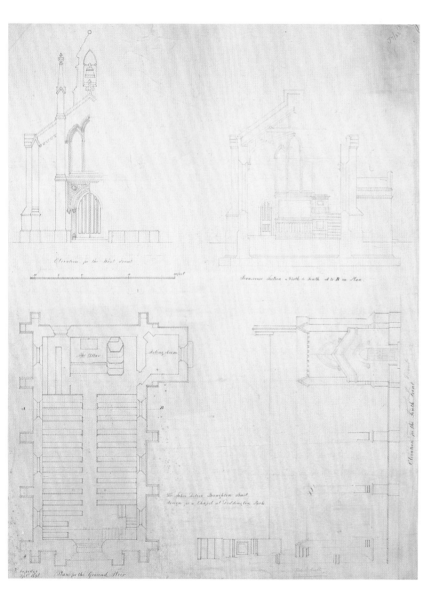

T HE chapel of ease which Lapidge
built for Sir Delves Broughton is
typical of the rather dull Gothic
churches in yellow stock brick
that formed Lapidge's main work.
These were the sort of churches that
Pugin was soon to sweep away.

The drawing, although unfinished,
shows how Lapidge set out to place
the salient elements of the building,
plan, elevations and section on a
single sheet of paper. His father had
been Capability Brown's assistant,
and Lapidge himself was appointed
Surveyor to the County of Surrey in
1824. He was elected a fellow of the
Institute of British Architects in 1838,
soon after it was founded. He is best
remembered, however, for the
crushing account his pupil George
Wightwick gave of him: 'I expected to
find a tutor: I found only an employer.
I thought to learn *great* things: I found
I had to act small ones. I had dreamed
of columnar splendours, arcaded
magnificence, of firmamental domes,
of "heaven-dictated spires": I found
economic contrivance and a parsimo-
nious minimum of decoration, for
cupolas, plain flat ceilings; for steeples
nothing more elevated than chimney-
tops.'

Lewis Vulliamy 1791-1871
Competition design for
Christ Church, Woburn Square,
Camden, London
105 Perspective, 1830
Pen with grey and blue washes
(635 × 415)

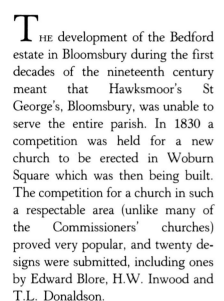

T HE development of the Bedford estate in Bloomsbury during the first decades of the nineteenth century meant that Hawksmoor's St George's, Bloomsbury, was unable to serve the entire parish. In 1830 a competition was held for a new church to be erected in Woburn Square which was then being built. The competition for a church in such a respectable area (unlike many of the Commissioners' churches) proved very popular, and twenty designs were submitted, including ones by Edward Blore, H.W. Inwood and T.L. Donaldson.

Vulliamy also prepared a Greek design, but it was the Gothic scheme which was chosen. Although this still owes much to the Gothic of the eighteenth century, Vulliamy's design with its bold spire contrasting with the restrained Georgian terraces around anticipates the ragstone churches that were such a feature of Belgravia, Pimlico and Kensington in the middle years of the century. Seating for 1,500 was provided, one-third of them free places, and in 1834 Vulliamy claimed that the church, which was still unfinished, would cost less than £8,000. In fact it cost £11,173, of which £5,097 came as a grant from the Commissioners. The drawing is inscribed *'Deo Gloria Patriae Decus'*, Vulliamy's pseudonym for the anonymous competition.

V URBAN ARCHITECTURE

Nowhere was the link between the rapidly expanding British economy and the architectural world clearer than in speculative urban building. Dizzy years of growth were followed by sudden crashes which could bankrupt even the most prosperous builder. The building trade would then stagnate for a year or more before slowly picking up strength leading to a boom, only for the bubble to burst again. Builders worked on credit and generally on a small scale, taking a building site on a peppercorn rent and selling on the remainder of the 99-year lease once the building was complete. Such men had no financial resources to support them in times of trouble. They were easily caught exposed with a finished building that nobody wanted to take off their hands.

War distorted the pattern of the economy during the first half of the Regency, although the underlying cycle remains clear. The period opens at a time of rapid growth. 1788 had seen a severe crash, but by 1790 that was a thing of the past, with brick production in the twelve months to the middle of that year higher than ever before. The textile industry was at a record level, harvests were good, incomes rising, interest rates falling. For a successful developer profits were enormous. Michael Searles, a south London surveyor, architect and developer whose scheme for fifty-eight houses off the Kent Road (106) was typical of his ambition to design on a large scale, must have had an income of about

£2,000 in 1792. The outbreak of war in 1793 together with a wet harvest hit the economy, removing the effective demand for new housing at the same time that credit for construction dried up. Brick production fell forty per cent in two years. Searles misjudged the situation, entering into a scheme for twenty-one large houses in the Blackheath Paragon, despite having five unsold houses on his hands from an earlier development. Only severe retrenchment and the sale of all his property prevented bankruptcy, and even then he was not able to meet his debts in full.

The decline continued until 1799, but then slowly improved again, with the next cycle running through to 1816, a cycle confused by the effects of war. These years were never easy, as S.P. Cockerell argued when accused of allowing shoddy workmanship in 1807: 'if I had pressed the builders to the extent of the power I possessed under their contracts, most of them must have failed, and the Foundling estate have been left in the condition of those estates in Bath, Bristol, and other places where from the effects of the war . . . whole acres remain in a state of ruin and desolation.' But houses were built, particularly in Bloomsbury and on the Portman estate (116-17), and by 1814 these overstocked the market at a time of rising costs of building materials and acute shortage of credit. In that year John Feltham could write in *The Picture of London, for 1815* 'at the time of writing the town is overbuilt, many thousands of houses in private

situations being unlet, and very numerous families engaged in building speculations have been ruined, besides 20,000 workmen being out of employment.'

These were difficult times in which to start London's greatest urban redevelopment, Nash's Regent Street, and its early years were dogged by bankruptcy. Economic distress prevented an immediate recovery after the war, but in 1819 the annual output of bricks exceeded a thousand million for the first time, and the bulk of Regent Street was complete by 1823. Abundant funds, a rising population and good economic conditions brought furious speculation. At the beginning of 1825 £10,000 could swiftly be raised to fund the building of St Bride's Avenue by Papworth (108). This was nothing to the £600,000 mooted for a new Mansion House Street or the £800,000 for a City of London Central Street, with both of which Papworth was involved. The crash when it came was dramatic. The younger Pugin, then thirteen, noted its course in his diary, beginning with a panic in the City on 28 November 1825 and then on 10 December a run on all the country banks. On 14 December James Morrison described London as being 'terror struck like a City surprised by an Earthquake'. Week after week during the first months of 1826 Pugin charted the number of bankruptcies, which reached as many as sixty a day in January and February. For the building trade the years to 1832 were years of almost unrelieved difficulty. Brick production did not manage to regain the same level until the late 1840s. But prosperity returned in the last years before Queen Victoria succeeded, with a new peak in 1836, allowing a new wave of development such as George Basevi's Pelham Crescent in 1833-40 (111-15).

Basevi's stucco elevations epitomise the Regency terraced house. In plan and basic layout this followed the pattern established in the early eighteenth century, but renewed attention was paid to the facade. In the late eighteenth century this had reached the summation of astylar restraint, as is shown in Searles's Kent Road scheme. The Regency saw a reaction against this with bowed or canted fronts added to some houses and a greater use of the orders on others, although few were as exuberant as Busby's unexecuted scheme for West Cliff Terrace in Brighton of about 1825 (109).

Like Busby's scheme for developing Brunswick Town (107) this was planned to be faced with stucco. Stucco is the classic Regency material, meant to give the appearance of stone but without its cost. Although used by the Adams in the 1770s and 1780s it was only with the invention of Roman cement in 1796 that stucco became common, especially after 1810 when the patent for Parker's Roman Cement ran out. All the great Regency developments after Regent Street are of stucco, but even before Pelham Crescent was completed in 1840 the tide was turning against it. The Reform Club, designed by Charles Barry in 1837, could have been in stucco or stone but the committee decided on stone despite an extra cost of nearly ten per cent. By the early 1840s stucco was being vehemently attacked as cheap and structurally deceptive. As in the changes in church building, it was the vigorous attacks in Pugin's *Contrasts* that heralded the end for what the Regency had held acceptable.

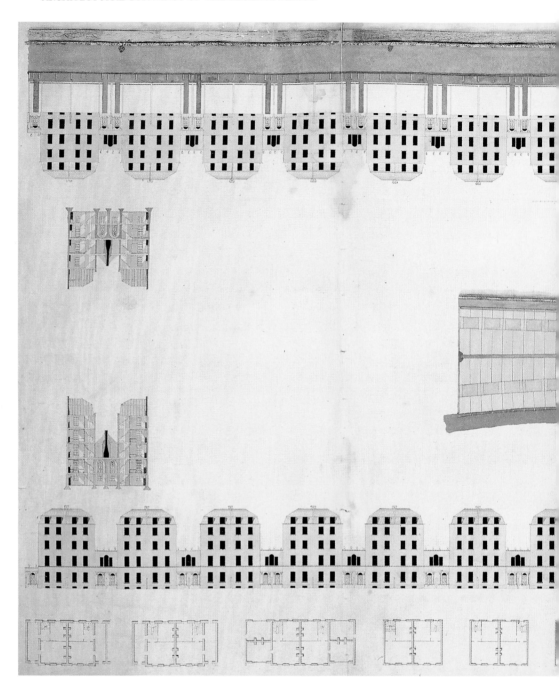

Michael Searles 1750-1813
Design for developing an estate of
58 houses off the Kent Road,
Southwark, London
106 Site plan with elevations,
sections and plans, n.d.
Pen and coloured washes
(620 × 985)

SEARLES drew up this ambitious scheme for Abraham and William Driver, two Quakers who had inherited land adjacent to the Kent Road in Southwark. The scheme was never executed and instead Searles built a terrace of thirteen houses, subsequently extended, called Surrey Place, with the rest of the site being laid out as Surrey Square.

By breaking up the conventional terrace into a series of semi-detached houses with two-storey linking bays Searles was attempting to get away from the standard speculative development and create a smarter image. He soon repeated this at Prince's Square, and it became a regular fea-

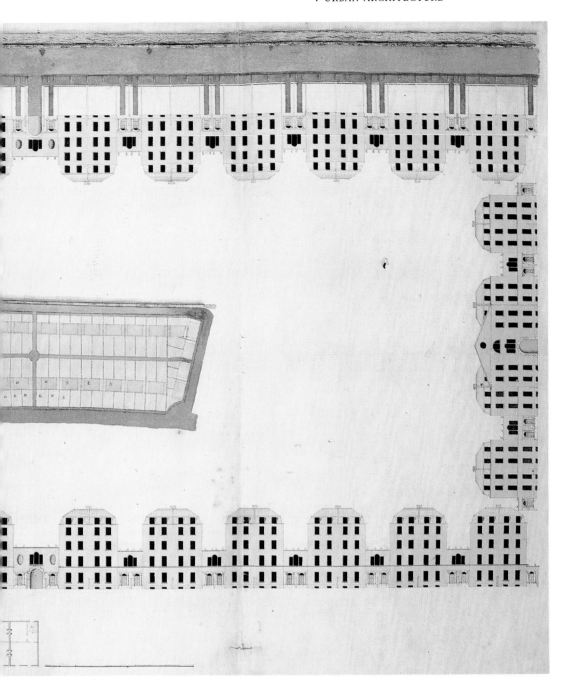

ture of his better developments. Although it was never built, the scheme demonstrates Searles's ability to consider developments on a large scale, something that he would later bring to fruition at the Southwark Paragon, the Circus, Greenwich and the Paragon, Blackheath.

The drawing is unparalleled in the large number of Searles drawings in the RIBA, and was clearly a presentation drawing intended to attract builders to take building sub-leases. As well as the basic layout and the elevations of all the street fronts, the drawing shows sections of representative houses and plans of each floor.

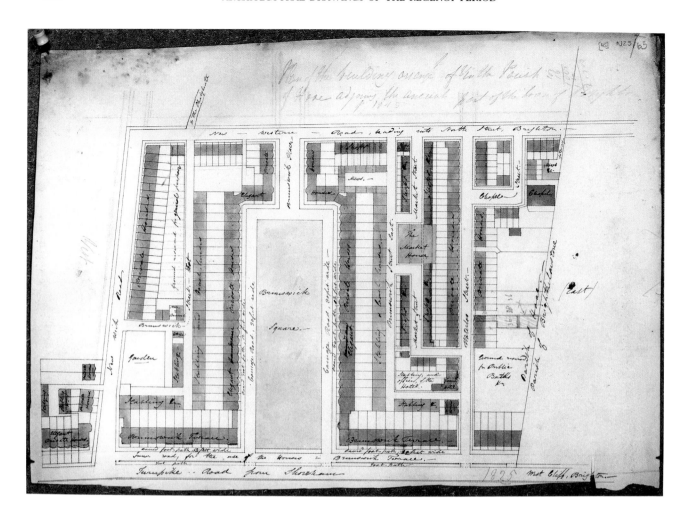

Charles Augustin Busby
1786-1834
Preliminary design for Brunswick
Square, Hove, East Sussex
107 Plan, 1825
Pen and wash (300 × 430)

Busby won the gold medal in his first year at the Royal Academy schools, but took time to set himself up as an architect. He even spent six years in America. On his return to England in 1820 he was unable to establish an independent practice and so moved to Brighton where he formed a partnership with Amon Henry Wilds, a local architect. Together they laid out Kemp Town to the east of Brighton from 1823. Independently, Busby also laid out Brunswick Town in Hove to the west from 1824. Although the land was owned by the Rev. Thomas Scutt, he played very little part in the development, and, as at Kemp Town, the prime mover was Thomas Kemp.

Busby was appointed surveyor in charge of Brunswick Town in 1832 on a salary of £40 a year.

This drawing shows Busby's design for the Brunswick estate close to completion. It was to be a self-contained township, based on a large central square, Brunswick Square, around which were to be gathered rows of smaller houses, mews, a chapel, a hotel, baths, a ballroom, a public house, shops and a market. Detailed drawings survive for almost every aspect of the development.

John Buonarotti Papworth
1775-1847
Design for St Bride's Avenue, Fleet
Street, City of London
108 Perspective, 1825
Pen and wash (645 × 480)

THE buildings in Fleet Street immediately to the north of St Bride's Church were badly damaged by fire on 14 November 1824. This opened up a view of St Bride's and the Corporation of London's Improvements Committee was petitioned to help purchase some of the damaged houses so that the view could be kept and a suitable approach to the church created. Papworth was called upon to design a new street on this axis, and an aquatint based on the drawing here was published on 28 January 1825 appealing for subscribers. Ten thousand pounds was raised and the foundation stone was laid in November by John Blades, the treasurer and chief mover of the scheme. Work continued until 1828.

For Papworth St Bride's Avenue was a rare chance to design on a relatively large scale, and it was considered the largest and most complete example of his work in London. It was typical of the many small Regency street alterations which cumulatively did much to improve the City. St Bride's Avenue has since been redeveloped.

Papworth's relationship with Blades is evidence of the wide range of his practice. He also remodelled the front of Blades's glassware shop, designed chandeliers and other objects for it, designed Brockwell Lodge and oversaw the development of Blades's Brockwell estate in south London until Blades's death in 1829.

Front Elevation of six Houses proposed to b

Charles Augustin Busby
1786-1834
Design for three terraced houses on
the West Cliff, Brighton, East Sussex
109 Elevation, *c.* 1825
Pen and coloured washes
(405 × 460)

Busby's early reputation for draughtsmanship which had led him to exhibit his first drawing at the Royal Academy at the age of fifteen and won him the gold medal there, is well reflected in this beautiful exam-

ple. Its other half, which is a mirror image, survives in a private collection. Few amongst his drawings match the quality here and it is unusual to find a design for speculative housing so treated. Sadly, the terrace was never built.

Although most Regency town houses remained wedded to the traditional austerity of the Georgian terrace there was a move towards a more picturesque treatment of facades. In the 1760s and 70s some architects, and in particular Sir Robert Taylor, had experimented with adding canted bays to the front of terraced houses but this never became standard. Some Regency

houses were built with bows to their main facade, primarily to take advantage of the view, as on the West Cliff where the houses faced the sea. Such bowed fronts are most commonly found in Regency resort towns like Brighton, Bath and Cheltenham, but in London a group of bow-fronted houses survives on Park Lane, looking over Hyde Park, and another on Birdcage Walk overlooking Green Park. Busby's design combines the bowed front with an elaborate use of canopied balconies, pilasters and acroteria cresting to create an urban architecture that can only be described as picturesque.

George Wightwick 1802-1872
Record drawing of the central section
of Athenaeum Terrace,
Plymouth, Devon
110 Plans and elevation, 1832-3
Pen with brown and grey washes
(410 × 315)

Aﬀer an uncomfortable period
as Soane's amanuensis and an unsuccessful attempt to establish a practice
in London, Wightwick moved to
Plymouth in 1829 where he formed a
partnership with John Foulston who
was then close to retirement. This
proved a success and Wightwick was
responsible for extensive work in Plymouth and Devonport and in the
neighbouring counties, earning up to
£1,800 a year.

Athenaeum Terrace was his first
Plymouth commission and must
have done much to establish his
reputation. This drawing shows only
the large central house built for Edward Jago; the terrace extended to
eleven houses, one of which was used
as offices for Messrs Wellcombe and
Jago, another, No. 3, Wightwick took
himself.

Although Soane employed Wightwick for only a few months as a
secretary his influence is clear in the
elevation, and in the interior where
Wightwick used pendentive domes.
It may also be that Wightwick picked
up the practice of making record
copies of his designs from Soane.
The RIBA has five volumes of his
drawings, done by his pupils, which
provide a very complete account of a
provincial architect's practice.

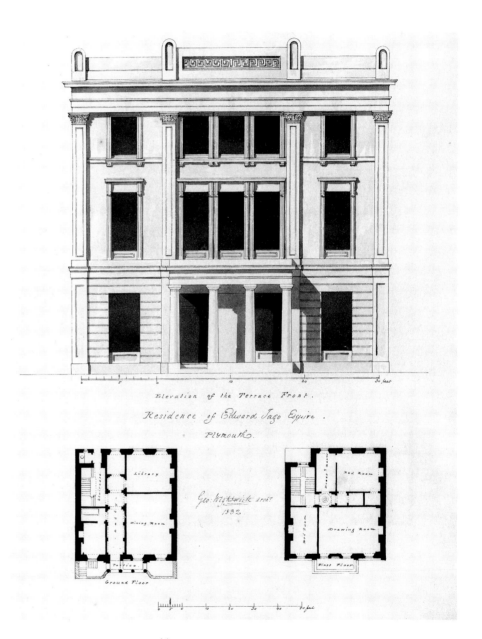

Elevation of the Terrace Front.

Residence of Edward Jago Esquire.

Plymouth.

Geo. Wightwick archt
1832.

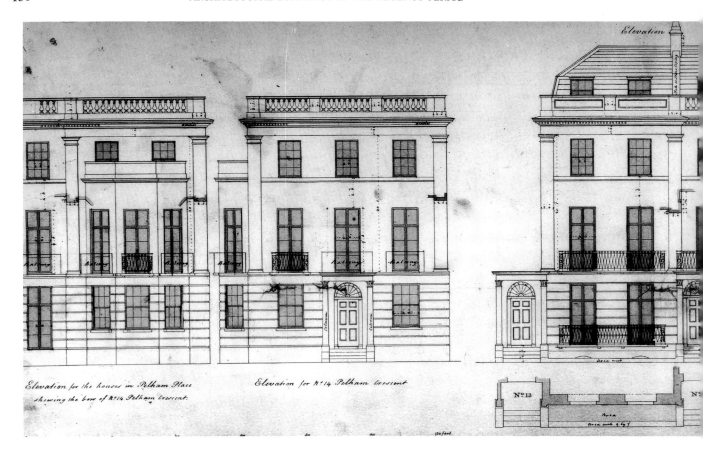

Elevation for the houses in Pelham Place
showing the bore of Nº14 Pelham Crescent.

Elevation for Nº14 Pelham Crescent

George Basevi 1794-1845
Contract drawings for Pelham
Crescent, Kensington and Chelsea,
London
111 Elevation, part-plan and part-
section, 1833
Pen and coloured washes
(320 × 965)

112 Site plan, 1833
Pen and coloured washes
(495 × 665)

Soane thought highly of Basevi

who was articled to him from 1811-
16. On returning from a three-year
tour of Italy and Greece he established an independent practice, becoming surveyor to the newly formed
Guardian Assurance Company in
1821. To this he subsequently added
the surveyorship of Smith's Charity
estate in Brompton in 1829 and later
that of the adjoining Thurloe estate.
With this solid base beneath him his
career flourished and he built half a
dozen churches, a dozen public
buildings and as many country
houses as well as supervising substantial developments in London before his career was cut short when he
fell to his death through the floor of

the belfry of Ely Cathedral in 1845.
　Although Basevi's designs for
Pelham Crescent and the adjoining
properties in Pelham Place and
Fulham Road lack the grandiosity of
his contemporary work in Belgrave
Square, they are good examples of
the restrained stucco houses that
characterised Regency London.
Basevi's scheme is not on the same
scale as Busby's at Brunswick Town
(107), but like Brunswick Town it is a
self-contained development with
substantial houses on Pelham Crescent and Pelham Place being com-
plemented by lesser houses on
Pelham Road and shops on the
Fulham Road.

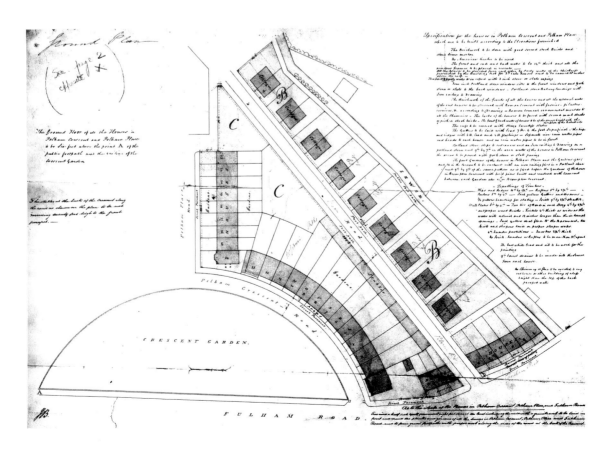

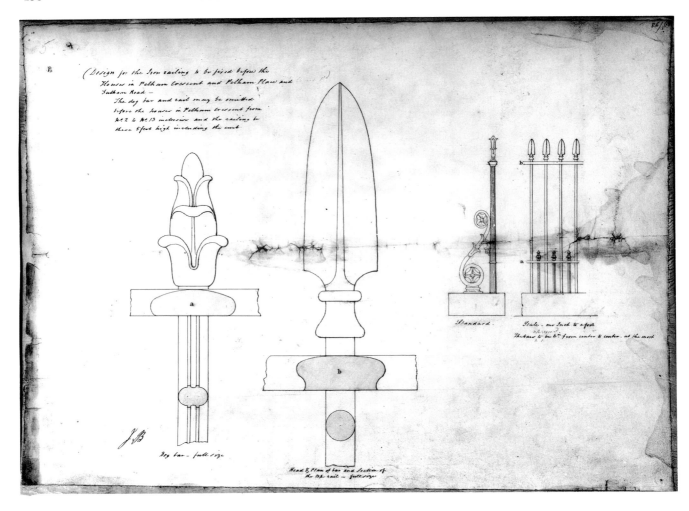

George Basevi 1794-1845
Contract drawings for Pelham Crescent,
Pelham Place and Fulham Road,
Kensington and Chelsea, London

113 Elevations and details of the
tops of the railings, 1833
Pen and coloured washes
(395 × 560)

114 Elevation, 1833
Pen and coloured washes (380 × 550)

115 Elevation and part-section, 1833
Pen and coloured washes (305 × 505)

Basevi laid plans of the proposed development before the trustees of Smith's Charity in 1829 and was paid £212 6s 9d for his trouble. Rates on the first fourteen houses in Pelham Crescent were paid for the first time in 1835 and the scheme was complete by 1840.

These drawings are part of a largely complete set of contract drawings for the Pelham Crescent development which survive, together with the original contract, in the RIBA. Two contracts were signed by the trustees and the builder James Bonnin in 1836 and 1838. The drawings provide every detail a speculative builder would have needed to build a terrace of houses, but while the appearance and layout of the houses were determined by the contract drawings, the structural details were left to the builder.

The designs for the shops are early examples of the nineteenth-century habit of having the shop front project from the building line of the house.

Pelham Crescent and Pelham Place survive, but the rest of the site has been redeveloped.

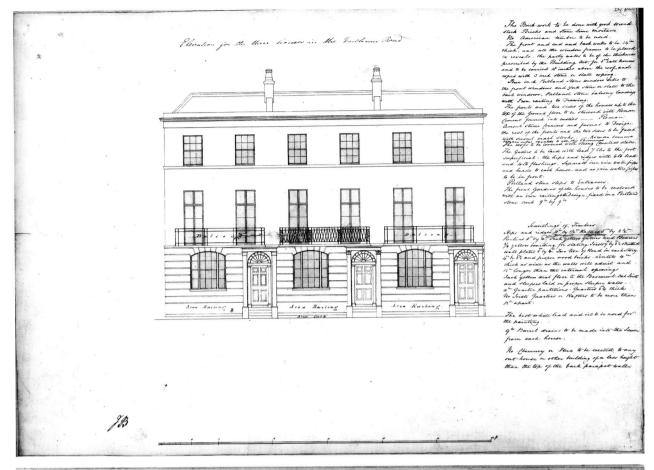

Elevation for the three Houses in the Fulham Road

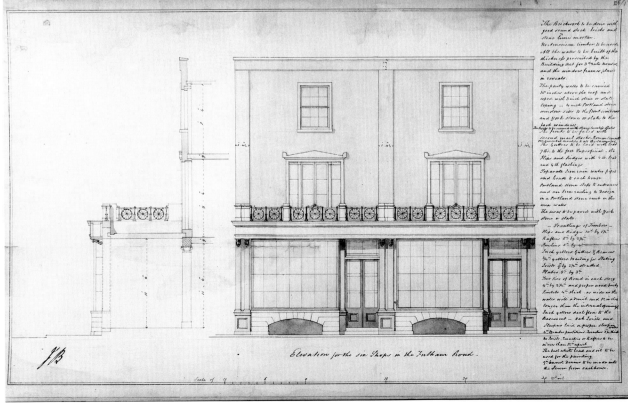

Elevation for the six Shops in the Fulham Road.

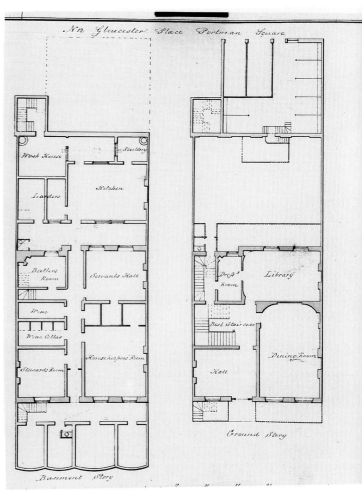

John Tasker 1738-1816
Survey drawing of No. 12 Gloucester
Place, Westminster, London
116 Plans, *c.* 1811
Pen with green and buff washes
(320 × 650)

Survey drawing of Nos. 12 and 13
Gloucester Place, Westminster,
London
117 Plan of the roof structure,
c. 1811
Pen with blue, green and buff washes
(320 × 530)

A BOUND volume of survey drawings of fourteen London houses
made by John Tasker in about 1811
survives in the RIBA. The volume
gives details of when the houses were
built (1808 for number 12), who was
the original leaseholder (Newcomb),
who had bought the lease when the
house had been built (Mrs Dorothy
Lawler) and when the lease would
fall in (1829). It was presumably
intended as a tool for efficient estate
management, and was typical of the
sort of work a London surveyor
would have had to do. As the drawings include the structural layout of
the main timbers and the decorative
treatment of the dome they were
probably taken from the original designs and were not specially executed
surveys.

No. 12 Gloucester Place, on the
west side of Portman Square has
been demolished, but was typical of
the substantial terraced houses built
in the latter decades of the eighteenth and early decades of the
nineteenth century. Such houses followed the pattern of the large Georgian town house codified on the
Grosvenor estate in the 1720s. At the
rear of the house, linked by a small
yard or garden is the mews with its
own access. The kitchens are in the
basement and the drawing room on
the first floor. Although 117 is inscribed *No. 12 Gloucester Place* it also
shows the roof structure of No. 13
which is identical except for the
curved rear wall.

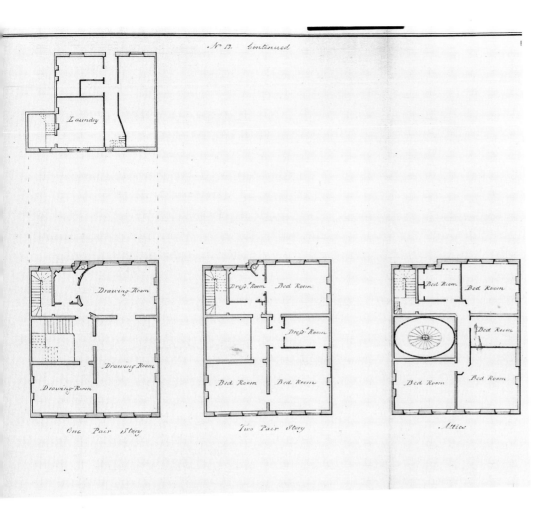

Nº 12. Continued

Laundry

Drawing Room

Drawing Room

Drawing Room

One Pair Story

Dresg. Room   Bed Room

Dresg. Room

Bed Room   Bed Room

Two Pair Story

Bed Room   Bed Room

Bed Room

Bed Room   Bed Room

Attics

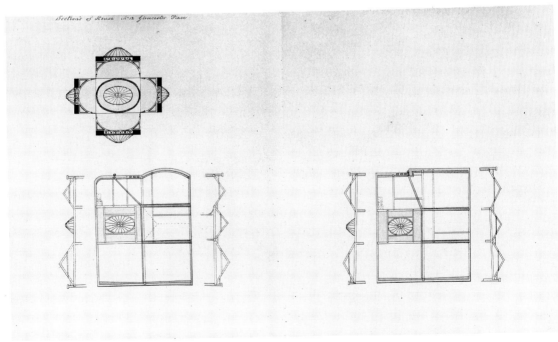

Sections of House Nº 12 Gloucester Place

John Baker *fl.* **1788-1807**
Survey drawings and alternative designs for re-fronting of No. 10 Fish Street Hill East, City of London
118 Plan of the site with adjacent properties, 1802
Pen and wash (405 × 255)

119 Three alternative elevations for the front facade, 1803
Pen and coloured washes (290 × 490)

120 Plans of the ground and first floors and plan showing the principal timbers to the first floor, 1802
Pen and coloured washes (285 × 405)

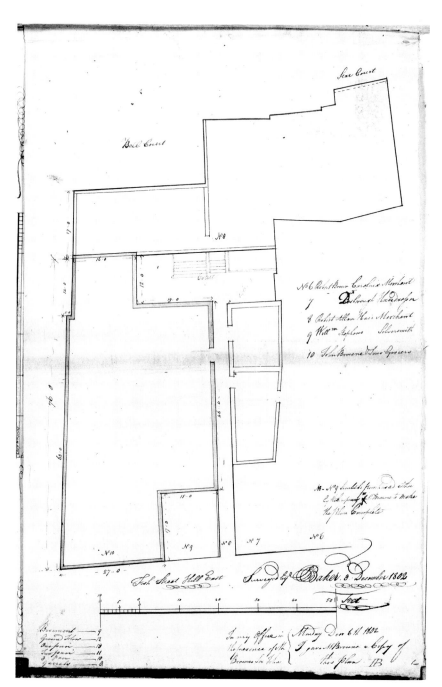

JOHN Baker was a surveyor operating in the City of London around the turn of the century. A booklet of his plans survives in the RIBA, the most important of which relate to the redevelopment of a house in Fish Street Hill in 1802-3 owned by the Haberdashers' Company. Baker was their surveyor, and his drawings reveal the process by which London property was redeveloped.

On 3 December 1802 he made a basic site plan showing the dimensions of the property and the names of the adjacent owners (118). Four days later he made plans of each floor of the house and of the structural timbers (120). On 1 January he sketched plans for rebuilding the house, and on 8 and 10 January he provided three alternative facades (119), each of which would fit the revised plan. This last drawing is inscribed *We approve this elevation (No. 1) and appoint Mr Baker as our Surveyor if we Erect the Building & should we not we will use our interest to recommend him to the party who shall build it. Johnson & Co. 2 Mar. 1804.*

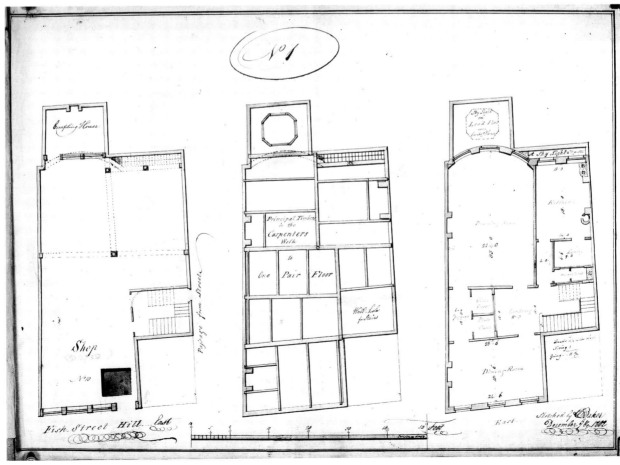

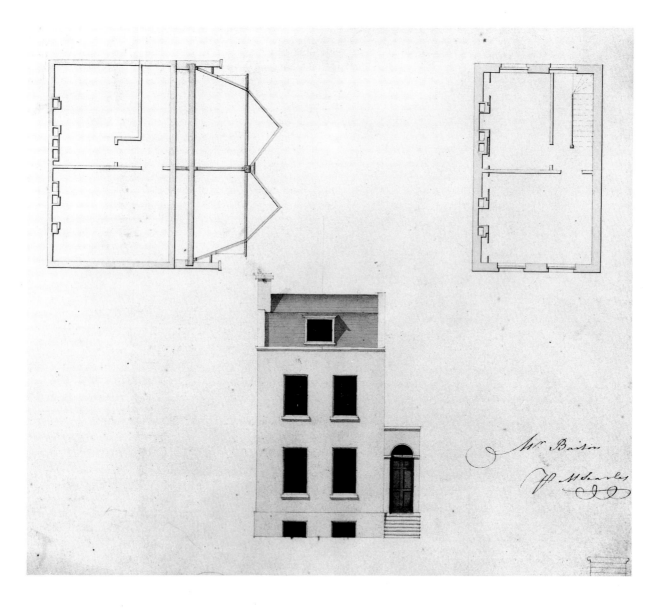

Michael Searles 1750-1813
Design for a small house for
Mr Barton
121 Plans of first and attic floors and
elevation, *c.* 1792
Pen and coloured washes
(255 × 265)

Searles was one of south London's most successful architects of speculative housing, building some of the most distinguished developments such as the Southwark and Blackheath Paragons. But this drawing reminds us that not all his houses were on that scale, for here is a design for a fourth-rate house, the very lowest level of urban building. It has no basement but two rooms on the ground floor, two more on the first floor and further accommodation in a mansard roof. Although mansard roofs are generally seen as modern additions to terraced houses they were often found in all classes of London Regency houses. Searles's houses generally have them. Mr Barton seems to have been one of Searles's suppliers as he was owed £23 2s in 1795.

The drawing shows the elevation and first-floor plan. For the mansard floor which has no windows set into the wall, a section of the timber structure is laid flat beside it to show where the windows would fall. Although it is only for a humble dwelling Searles's drawing is well laid out and attractively coloured.

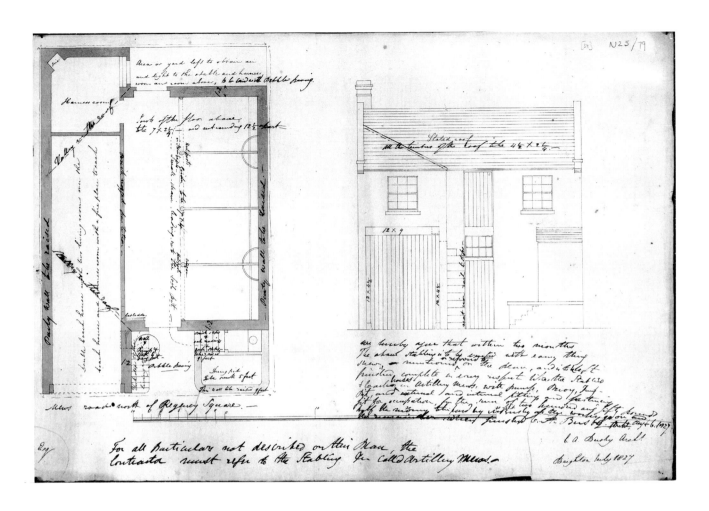

**Charles Augustin Busby
1786-1834**
Contract drawing for a mews in
Regency Mews, Brighton,
East Sussex
122 Elevation and plan, 1827
Pen and wash (300 × 445)

Most substantial Regency terraced houses were built with a mews
at the rear, and one of the marks of
the intended standing of a development was the number of its houses
that had mews. At Brunswick Town

Busby provided mews for all the
main houses in Brunswick Square
and Brunswick Place but not for the
lesser streets. Regency Mews served
Regency Square, built in 1818-28,
which was not designed by Busby
and had nothing to do with Brunswick Square.

Busby first drew out the plan and
elevation in July 1827. Further information for the builder was then
added to the neat drawing, when the
builder inscribed *We hereby agree
that within two months/ The above
stabling is to be erected with every
thing/ shewn, mentioned or referred to
on the plan, and is to be left/ finished
complete in every respect like the*

*Stabling/ and Coach houses in Artillery
Mews, with pump, Privy, Dung/-Pit,
and external and internal fittings and
fastenings/ fit for occupation, for the
sum of two hundred and fifty pounds/
half the money to be paid by Mr Busby
as the works go on and/ the remainder
when finished.* It thus moved from
being a design drawing to a contract
drawing.

Mews were at the lowest end of
the scale of Georgian urban
architecture, and the extreme simplicity of this facade should be compared with the careful elaboration of
Busby's contemporary design for a
terrace on the West Cliff (109).

VI COMMERCIAL BUILDINGS

THE Regency was a time of dramatic expansion for the British economy, but that is barely reflected in the RIBA Drawings Collection. While it is hard to make a choice from the vast selection of drawings for public buildings, houses and churches, the range of drawings of commercial buildings is limited.

This is partly because of the nature of the client. While landed families like the Wyndhams of Dinton (32-9) who commissioned country houses have traditionally kept their papers, and parish councils have had to maintain parochial records which might include the original designs for the church like those of St John, Hoxton (85-96), firms who commissioned commercial buildings seldom achieved great longevity. The exceptions were the dock companies, but their extensive collections of drawings have not come to the RIBA.

Equally significant is the nature of the drawing. Public buildings, country houses and churches were considered to be of general architectural interest. Commercial buildings seldom were. There was little need for the handsome perspectives and presentation drawings that attract the collector's eye for buildings that were considered purely functional. Still, it is remarkable how few drawings for commercial buildings do survive. It must be significant that of the drawings illustrated in this chapter a high proportion either are record drawings — Repton's (123), Wightwick's (128-9) and Edwards's (135-8) — were presented by architects to the newly formed Institute of British Architects soon after they were executed — Fowler's (130-2), Smith's (140) and Edwards's again — or survived in architects' collections — Rickman's (124), Busby's (127) and Papworth's (133-4). An unconscious bias over 150 years has winnowed the 'fine' from the commercial architectural drawings.

Banking flourished during the Regency, and it was not only Soane's Bank of England that bore architectural witness to that prosperity. According to R.D. Richards's *The Early History of Banking in England* (1929) there were 780 private banks in London in 1826, sixty of them in London. Most of these, like Hopkinson's Bank (123), followed the basic domestic pattern of the terraced house, and the same was true of offices. But even before the end of the Regency banks and offices were assuming their own distinctive form, a form often marked by architectural elaboration previously reserved for public buildings, as the Corinthian portico of Rickman and Hutchinson's Birmingham Bank shows (124).

Shops remained faithful to the domestic pattern; the main change there came with the invention of larger panes of glass, allowing shop fronts like Busby's (127) to achieve a lightness that appeared all glass. Full-length plate-glass windows were not to come for some time. But while most shopping was carried out in conventional shops, the Regency also saw the introduction of the bazaar, starting with the two-level Soho Bazaar in Soho Square in 1816, where, unlike a conventional shop, a range of goods were sold. The same year saw the opening of the Royal Opera Arcade, the first of three Regency arcades, where a selection of shops were linked under a covered walk. Sadly, there are no good drawings of bazaars or arcades in the RIBA, but a related phenomenon, the great covered market is well represented.

Covered markets were an important feature of most Georgian urban developments, but they were usually small in scale and few survive. However, the Regency saw many more built both in provincial cities and county towns and in London. The greatest of these was Fowler's Hungerford Market (130-2), designed to serve the whole of London's West End with fish, meat, fruit, vegetables, flowers and grain. It was not a commercial success and has gone but Fowler's Covent Garden survives as a pale shadow of what it must have been like.

Today the finest achievement of Regency architecture would probably be seen to be the great series of docks and warehouses built in London and other great ports like Liverpool. These were stimulated by the growing value of trade which doubled from £34 million in the decade between 1790 and 1800. The Dock Act of 1799 marked the opening of seven years of vigorous dock construction which saw the erection of the West India Docks, the London Docks, East India Docks and the Grand Surrey

Canal Company Docks. Some of these survive but all too many have been demolished in recent years. There are no drawings for these in the RIBA, but Edwards's Lion Brewery (135-8), though on a relatively small scale, gives an idea of how they were built.

The increasing scale of the industrial revolution demanded larger and larger buildings both for manufacture and warehousing. It was to meet this demand that Samuel Wyatt built the great Albion Mill in Southwark in 1783-6. But Wyatt designed the mill with a conventional timber structure, and in 1791 it burnt down in one of the most dramatic fires London had seen. The result was a turning-point

as architects and engineers realised that they must find a way of making such buildings safe from fire. The answer lay in cast-iron which Jebediah Strutt used in Derby the following year for the first time in a major structural capacity. In 1796 Charles Bage used iron beams for the first time. Thereafter the use of iron increased rapidly and was a routine structural material by the 1820s. Such buildings were still built with load-bearing brick walls. It was only after 1830 that the first steps were made towards building fully skeletal outer structures. In the meantime conventional timber structures continued to be used, as by Papworth at Grosvenor Basin in 1830 (133-4).

Advances in the understanding of cast-iron were also reflected in bridge design, something that had become of increasing importance as communications were improved during the eighteenth century. Bridges's design for spanning the Avon Gorge, Clifton, Bristol (139) of 1793 makes clear the restrictions of conventional technology, but the Smiths' chain bridge at Dryburgh of 1817 pointed the way forward (140). Although a design fault caused the bridge to collapse soon after it was put up this was modified and the resurrected bridge was a success. By the end of the Regency Brunel had even devised a way successfully to span the Avon Gorge.

George Stanley Repton 1786-1858
Record drawing of Hopkinson's
Bank, No. 3 Regent Street,
Westminster, London
123 Ground and first floor plan and
elevation, 1817-18
Pen and wash (475 × 345)

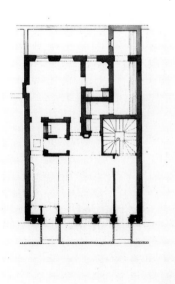

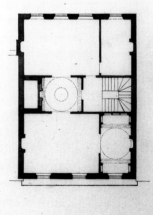

Mᴇssʀs Hopkinson, bankers and army agents, were established at No. 3 Regent Street in 1820. The development of Regent Street between 1812 and 1826 was a remarkable achievement. John Nash designed various of the facades but many of the buildings were the work of different architects. This lower part of Regent Street was developed between 1817 and 1820 when G.S. Repton was still in Nash's office but already designing on his own account. As this drawing is on paper watermarked 1829 it must be a later record drawing, unless it was intended for a proposed publication which was never completed.

The design of the bank reveals its domestic origins, and like contemporary shops the upper floors are given over to living quarters. However, the dignified baseless Doric colonnade and relatively small windows make it clear that this was not a shop.

The door on the right gave access to the partners' staircase and to the main banking hall. That on the left was for customers, allowing them into the body of the bank where they were separated from the clerks by a counter. A short top-lit lobby gave access to the manager's office with its own closet beyond. At the rear, behind the staircase, was a long narrow room with a continuous writing desk for clerks. The bank was demolished early this century.

**Thomas Rickman 1776-1841 and
Henry Hutchinson 1800-1831**
Design for the Birmingham Banking
Company, Waterloo Street,
Birmingham
124 Perspective of the entrance front,
1830
Pen on tracing paper (445 × 640)

RICKMAN had little to do with the design of the Birmingham Banking Company's building. News of the possible commission was brought on 3 November 1830, on the eve of his departure from Birmingham. Charles Edge, who had established himself in Birmingham in 1827 and who was rapidly becoming one of the city's leading architects, was also asked to provide a scheme. Rickman visited his partner Henry Hutchinson on 5 November and satisfied himself that he had made a very good arrangement for the bank before setting off on an extensive tour of work in hand. On his return on 20 November he heard that the commission had been decided in their favour.

By contrast with Hopkinson's Bank of 1818 (123), the Birmingham Banking Company's building has a civic rather than a domestic air. The increasing importance of finance is reflected in the grand Corinthian portico, which in the eighteenth century would have been thought more appropriate for a church or palace. There was some confusion over this in the competition. The original requirement had been for a handsome building, but other reports spoke of the need for a plain building with no money wasted. This seems to have arisen from infighting within the bank, with those who wanted a handsome design clearly winning.

The building still exists but was altered in about 1870 by the addition of an entrance on the corner.

The Hotel at Carnarvon

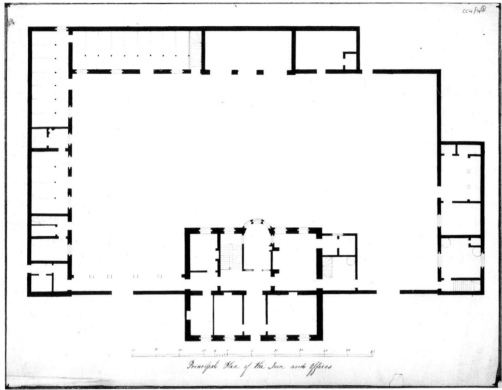

cc4/14

Principal Plan of the Inn and Offices

Robert Jones *fl.* **1823**
Design for the Uxbridge Hotel,
Caernarvon, Gwynedd
125 Front elevation, n.d.
Pen and wash (235 × 610)

126 Ground plan, n.d.
Pen (395 × 525)

Tʜᴇ German traveller Prince Puckler-Muskau was more impressed by the comfort of British hotels than by anything else when he visited England in the 1820s. By the second decade of the nineteenth century an efficient network of inns covered the country helped by the rapid improvement of the roads with turnpikes, and by the increasing sophistication of the coaching system.

Caernarvon, which in the eighteenth century would have been considered remote, inaccessible and of little interest, profited from the boom in tourism that developed thanks to the growth of picturesque sensibility married with the improved roads and coaches. Its medieval castle was a subject of great interest, and the town lay close to the romantic landscape of Snowdonia.

Drawings for the Uxbridge Hotel are included in a larger deposit relating to the nearby Plas Newydd estate of the Marquess of Anglesey. It is a typical example of the hotels developed to cater for this new, genteel trade. It has extensive stabling and the small bay-windowed room at the rear of the main block of the hotel would have held the bar whose strategic position opposite the front door, by the stairs and with a bow window looking out into the stable-yard, would have ensured quick service to any part of the hotel.

Charles Augustin Busby
1786-1834
Design for a shop front probably
on the Western Road, Hove,
East Sussex
127 Elevation, *c.* 1825
Pen and coloured washes
(350 × 620)

I<small>N</small> *Sketches by Boz*, published in 1836, Charles Dickens talks of the sudden passion for plate-glass that had appeared about six years earlier. Glazed shop windows had been uni-versal since the mid-eighteenth cen-tury, but typical small-paned Geor-gian windows began to give way to larger panes in the first decades of the nineteenth century. Technical reasons prevented full-length win-dows, and in 1828 panes were about four feet long and never more than five feet high. It was only in the 1840s that larger windows were in-troduced.

The collection of Papworth draw-ings in the RIBA includes large num-bers of shop designs, and as a prolific London architect they were obvious-ly an important part of his practice. An urban architect like Busby in Brighton would often have been cal-led upon to design shop windows which were considered ephemeral and were frequently changed. Regent Street was designed so that the shop fronts were not structural and could be changed at will. As a result few such shop fronts survive.

Busby's design with its delicate pattern of glazing bars is a particular-ly handsome example, and was prob-ably for a row of shops intended to serve Brunswick Town (107). The elegant frieze of acroteria and Greek-key patterned ironwork make it a good example of the way that Gre-cian ornament was adapted to architectural use.

Houses and Shop of Dabb, Rundle and Brown, Old Town, and Treville Streets, Plymouth.

General Elevation towards Treville Street

George Wightwick 1802-1872
Record drawings for two houses and shops for Dabb, Rundle and Brown, Plymouth, Devon
128 Elevation, *c.* 1833
Pen with blue, brown and grey washes (315 × 410)

129 Plan and section, *c.* 1833
Pen with blue, brown and grey washes (315 × 410)

THE Regency shop grew in-creasingly sophisticated, and Dabb, Rundle and Brown's drapery busi-ness was built on a large scale taking advantage of its corner site. With windows running down the whole of one side of the shop it would have been bathed in light. The windows were designed with a *Stage for Goods* to allow displays. Most of the space was given over to the upper or drap-ery shop with parallel rows of coun-ters and shelves behind. Beyond was the office and a staircase leading to the show room above, with access down to the basement, and a small closet under the stairs for a clerk. In the rear was the lower or cloth shop with the stairs leading to the private apartments beyond. Shop interiors have always been seen as transient creations, frequently altered, and so it is unlikely that any Regency shop interior remains intact. Thus Wight-wick's record drawing is a useful record of the workings of such a shop. Few architectural drawings sur-vive for shop interiors, although there are more for shop fronts.

Dabb, Rundle and Brown's shop sat at the junction of Old Town Street and Treville Street, but no longer exists. Treville Street has been obliterated, as has much of Old Town Street.

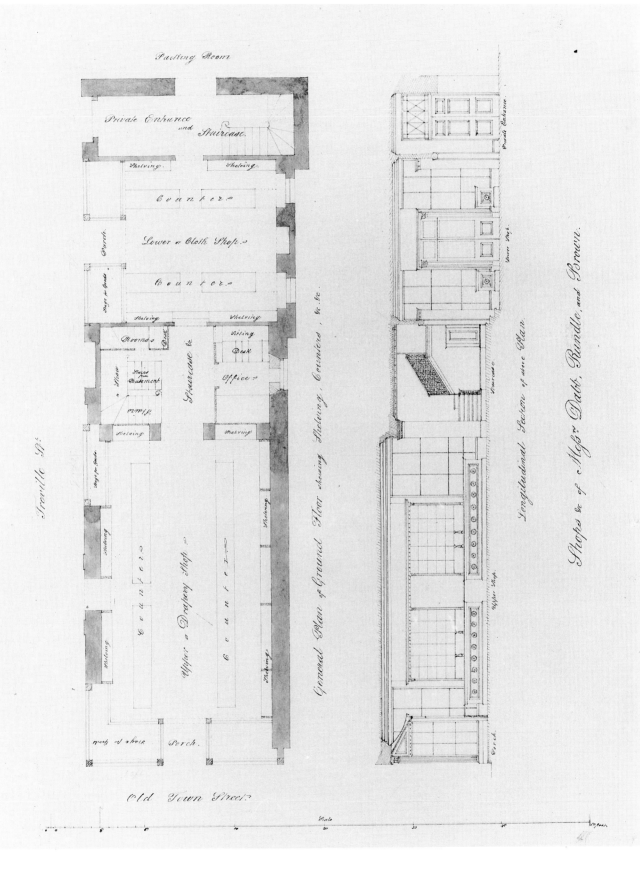

Packing Room

Private Entrance and Staircase.

Shelving. Shelving.

Counters

Lower or Cloth Shops

Counters

Shelving Shelving

Rooms Desk Siting

Staircase &c. Desk

Stairs Basement Office

Shelving Shelving

Upper or Drapery Shop

Counters

Counters

Shelving

Porch.

Trenville St.

Old Town Street.

General Plan of Ground Floor shewing Shelving, Counters, &c.

Longitudinal Section of one Plan.

Shops &c. of Messrs Dabb, Bundle, and Brown.

Scale

Charles Fowler 1792-1867
Design for Hungerford Market,
Charing Cross, Westminster,
London
130 Perspective sketch of the
interior, 1831
Pencil and sepia wash (175 × 145)

131 Perspective of the lower court,
1831
Watercolour (385 × 540)

Drawing made for the engraver
132 Plan and view of the metal roof
in the centre of fish market, 1836
Pen (230 × 300)

Hungerford Market was rebuilt between June 1831 and July 1833 at a total cost of £210,000. It was divided into three areas which, because of the lie of the land, were on different levels: the upper two selling fruit and vegetables or meat and poultry, and the lower court fish. At first this was open (131), but it was almost immediately given an innovative metal shelter with cast-iron columns and zinc roof (132). Fowler lectured the Institute of British Architects on the roof in 1836, his text being subsequently printed in the first volume of the Institute's *Transactions*, and it was for this occasion that fifty copies of the engraving were printed. Fowler then gave the original to the IBA.

The contrast between the central hall with its arcades and timber roof that seem to be inspired by an early-Christian basilica and the advanced engineering of the fish market roof is remarkable. Sadly, the market was not a commercial success and was demolished in 1862 to make way for Charing Cross station.

LOWER · COVRT · OF · HVNGERFORD · MARKET ·

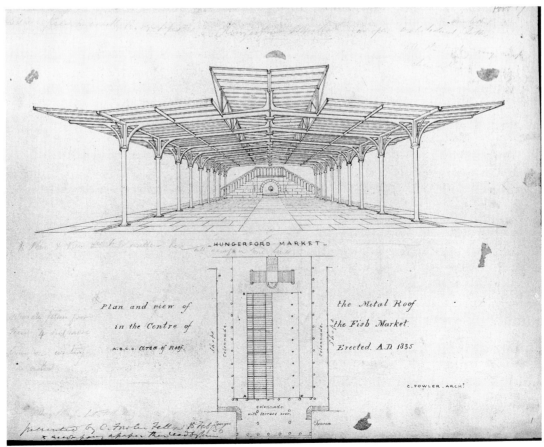

· HUNGERFORD · MARKET ·

Plan and view of
in the Centre of
A.B.C.D. *Area of Roof.*

the Metal Roof
the Fish Market.
Erected. A.D. 1835

C. FOWLER. ARCH!

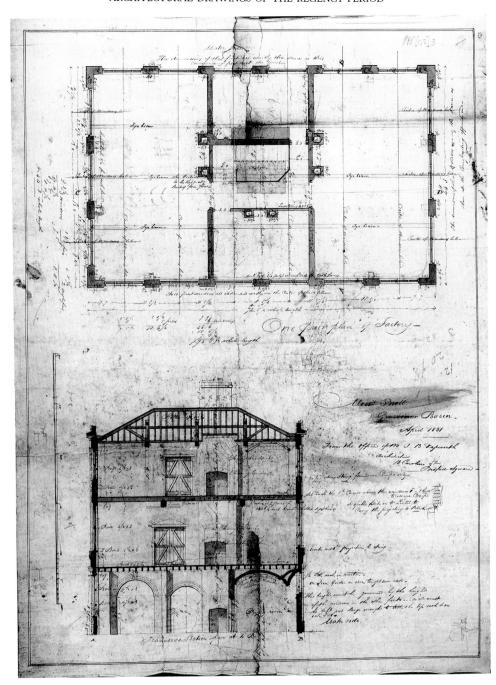

John Buonarotti Papworth
1775-1847
Design for a factory for W. & E. Snell,
Grosvenor Basin, Westminster, London

133 First floor plan and
transverse section, 1831
Black and red pen with
coloured washes (620 × 465)

134 Front and side elevations, 1831
Black and red pen with
yellow and sepia washes
(610 × 455)

Papworth's connection with Messrs William and Edward Snell, upholsterers and cabinetmakers, went back to 1815. In 1822-3 he had made repairs to William Snell's house in Berkeley Square, as well as altering the firm's premises. He also made designs for their furniture. In 1830 Papworth designed new workshops and a house for Edward Snell

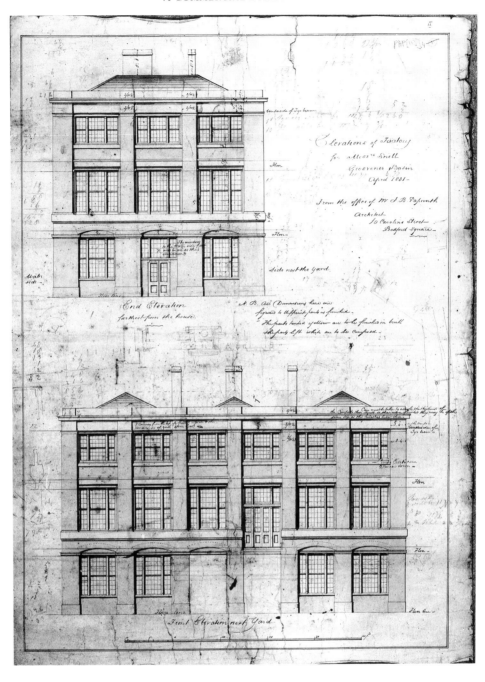

on the west side of Belgrave Road, by Eccleston Bridge. This was part of a new light industrial area served by the Grosvenor Canal (later replaced by Victoria Station) which had been built in 1823-6. The canal made for cheap and easy transport of materials and was soon surrounded by wharves, warehouses and mills, particularly serving the building trade.

One side of the Snells' works faced the water.

The factory was demolished in 1860-2 when the construction of Victoria Station led to the widening of Eccleston Bridge.

Unlike contemporary warehouses such as the Lion Brewery (135-8), Snell's workshops were built along traditional structural lines with load-bearing brick walls. There was no use of cast-iron columns. However, while a warehouse had no great need for light, a factory did — so that the workmen could see what they were doing — and Papworth's design has a high ratio of window to wall.

The drawings are closely annotated with dimensions and other information for the builder.

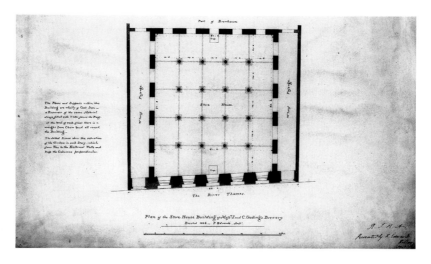

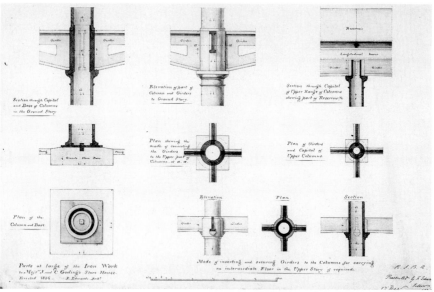

Francis Edwards 1784-1857
Record drawings of a storehouse at
the Lion Brewery, Belvedere Road,
Lambeth, London
135 Plan, 1836
Pen and coloured washes
(360 × 520)

136 Details of the ironwork, 1836
Pen and coloured washes
(360 × 520)

Although many of its contemporaries were larger, the Lion Brewery storehouse was one of the most handsome, owing this to its prominent site on the south bank of the Thames, where it formed a distinctive advertisement.

The degree of architectural ornament is unusual, and the facade owes more to Palladian domestic architecture than to contemporary warehouses. In fact the facade does not relate well to the floor levels behind. The basement floor has the highest ceiling level. The first floor, which from the outside appears to be a noble *piano nobile*, has the lowest ceiling which cuts into the top of the window. The articulation of the land front is no less elaborate, with a portico and twinned Doric pilasters. In its basic design the storehouse seems to show the influence of Edwards's former master Soane and his unexecuted scheme for the central section of East India House.

The layout and structural design of the warehouse is typical of many, with a regular grid of cast-iron columns supporting cast-iron beams. Protection against fire was a major reason for such a design, as was the need to get the maximum loading on to a given area. Further fire protection was provided by the large shallow water tank formed in the roof.

Elevation of the River Front of the Store House Building
Erected for Mess's J and C. Goding 1836, F. Edwards, Arch't

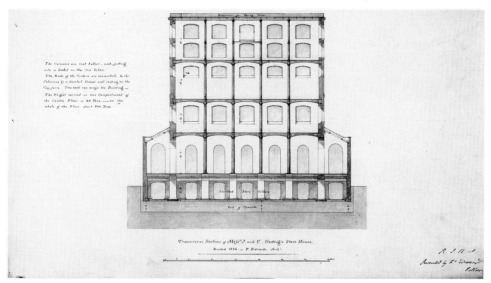

Transverse Section of Mess's J. and C. Goding's Store House.
Erected 1836 - F. Edwards, Arch't.

Francis Edwards 1784-1857
Record drawings of a storehouse at
the Lion Brewery, Belvedere Road,
Lambeth, London
137 Elevation of the river front, 1836
Pen and coloured washes (360 × 520)

138 Transverse section, 1836
Pen and coloured washes (360 × 520)

Edwards's practice had a strongly commercial slant, although his first significant commission was for the church of St John the Baptist, Hoxton (85-96). He was responsible for all the building and engineering works of the Imperial Gas Works Company from its incorporation in 1823. He was also much employed in arbitrations and valuations. Messrs Goding and Co., for whom he built the Lion Brewery Storehouse, were among his best clients. As well as designing the Lion Brewery in Lambeth (of which the storehouse was the dominant feature), he made additions to two other breweries owned by the firm in Knightsbridge and Golden Square, and built several public houses for them. In 1837 he built a house for Thomas Goding in St George's Place, Hyde Park Corner, London, and in 1840-7 he completed Wellington Square on the King's Road, London, for him.

These drawings were among the earliest to enter the collection, in 1838, and may well have been made for presentation. They are carefully coloured with brick in pink, iron in blue, wood, found only on the ground floor, in brown and the bed of concrete that formed the foundation in light brown. The set is completed by a longitudinal section.

The storehouse was demolished in 1949 to make way for the Royal Festival Hall, but the Coade stone lion was saved and re-erected on the Embankment by County Hall.

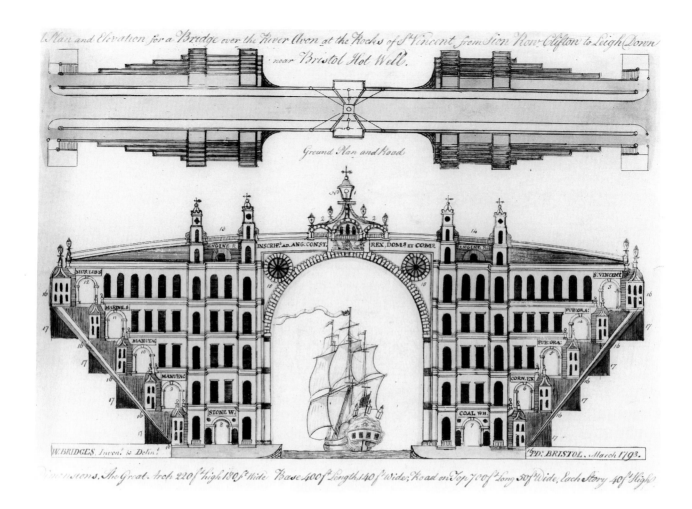

W. Bridges *fl.* **1793**
Design for a bridge over the Avon
at Clifton, Bristol
139 Plan and elevation, 1793
Pen and coloured washes
(275 × 375)

ONE thousand pounds was bequeathed to the City Guild of Bristol in 1735 to be left to accumulate at compound interest until it had reached £10,000 when it was to be used to build a bridge across the gorge at Clifton. Bridges's scheme was one of the earliest proposals, but it was only in 1829-36 that Isambard Kingdom Brunel's suspension bridge made it possible to span the gorge.

Bridges's design hardly seems worthy of serious consideration, but he meant it seriously for he had it engraved and printed a proposal. His answer to the problem was to narrow the gap as much as possible by building an enormous substructure, and then span it with a conventional bridge 220 ft high and 180 ft wide. The cost of the substructure was to be financed by letting off different levels. On the lowest level were to be stone and coal wharves, above were to be a corn exchange and factories with a museum and library and, most remarkable of all, a church on top. The design tried to use standard eighteenth-century building techniques to solve a problem that would only be resolved by Brunel's innovating genius. Even had the scheme been practical, 1793, the year war broke out with France, would have made such a major project impossible.

Nothing else is known of Bridges.

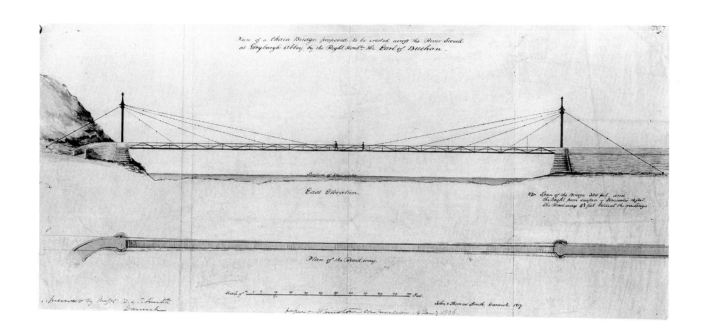

John Smith 1782-1864 and
Thomas Smith 1785-1857
Design for Dryburgh Bridge, Borders
140 Plan and elevation, 1817
Pen and watercolour (275 × 610)

Dryburgh Bridge was the first chain bridge to be built in Britain. It was a pedestrian bridge costing £560 with a span of 261 ft built in 1817 for the Earl of Buchan at Dryburgh Abbey. The following year it proved the first chain bridge to be blown down. The Smiths rebuilt it the same year but to a slightly modified design and at a further cost of £240. It has since been demolished.

The Smiths were local builders in Darnick, Borders, who showed a particular interest in bridges, but whose innovatory techniques were not always successful. The bridge carrying the drive to Bowhill over the Ettrick at Fauldshope, Borders, collapsed, and that over the Tweed at Ashiesteel initially failed.

The Smiths explained their actions in a paper read to the Institute of British Architects on 4 January 1836, soon after the Institute was founded, which was published in the first volume of its *Transactions*. Following the lecture this drawing was presented to the Institute which had resolved to form a library to which 'it is hoped, may be added manuscripts of a similar description, to be deposited for the inspection of all members, and drawings illustrative practically and theoretically of the art, in its widest application.'

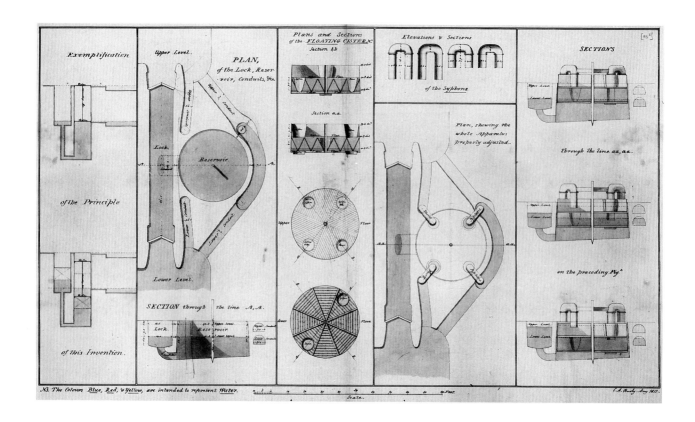

Charles Augustin Busby
1786-1834
Design for a canal lock
141 Plans and sections, 1813
Pen and coloured washes
(390 × 660)

Busby, like some other Regency architects including his master Daniel Alexander, described himself as an architect-engineer, and the Regency was a time of significant structural advances. This design for a canal lock with a complex series of syphons was never executed and the following year Busby left for America, only returning six years later. There is no evidence that he built any locks, but during his pupillage Alexander was building the London Docks, and so he would have had experience in the problems of lock design.

Despite the vast numbers of docks built and the thousands of miles of canal dug, this is one of the few Regency drawings relating to transport in the collection. Admittedly the growth of the canal network did not generate the volume of building that was to come with the railways, but it did stimulate demand, particularly for warehouses. These, though, were generally designed by company surveyors not independent practices, and therefore few have come to the RIBA.

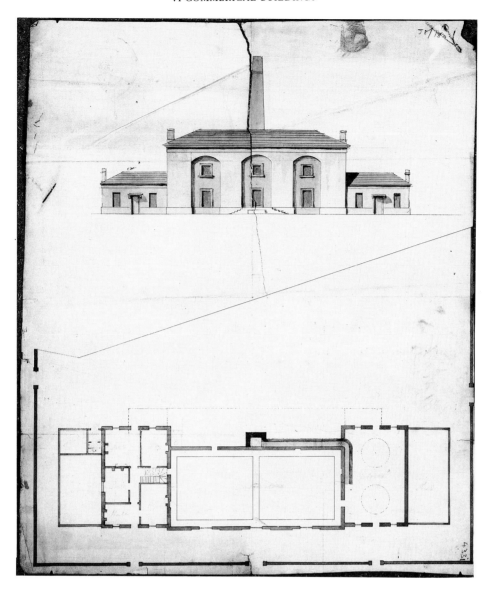

John William Hiort 1772-1861
Design for a gas house
142 Plan and elevation, *c.* 1814
Pen and wash (400 × 345)

HIORT was a loyal functionary of the Office of Works for forty-five years, becoming assistant clerk in 1793, resident clerk in 1805 and chief examining clerk in 1815. His Swedish parentage may have recommended him to Sir William Chambers who

was born in that country, but his introduction was through Charles Craig, one of the three principal officers of the Office of Works, whose private office he entered in 1787. Government service meant that Hiort was not allowed to develop a private practice, and apart from a few works at Claremont House, Surrey, where he acted as architect for Princess Charlotte before her premature death he designed little. It was on him that the main body of administration at the Office of Works fell during the surveyorship of James Wyatt.

It was in this official capacity that he designed this gas house for which an estimate entitled *Gass House in the Park* survives with the drawings. Presumably the park referred to is one of the London parks, the building would appear to be too large for private use, and so is unlikely to have been intended for Claremont. The centre part of the building was to hold the gasometers, to the right were the retorts, and on the left the manager's house and office. The estimated cost was £4,398.

SELECT BIBLIOGRAPHY

British Library, Add Ms 37793-37802, Rickman timebooks.

RIBA Ms Coc, Cockerell Diaries.

RIBA Ms Rickman Diaries.

RIBA Ms SaT, Six Lectures by Thomas Sandby.

RIBA Ms SmK 1-2 Smirke Papers.

RIBA Ms Wig/1/2 George Wightwick, 'The Life of an Architect'.

Sir John Soane's Museum, Soane Mss.

A. Barry, *The Life and Works of Sir Charles Barry*, London, 1867.

A.T. Bolton, *Architectural Education a Century Ago*, London, nd.

A.T. Bolton, *The Portrait of Sir John Soane*, London, 1927.

W. Bonwitt, *Michael Searles*, London, 1987.

R. Brown, *The Principles of Practical Perspective*, London, 1815.

A.K. Cairncross and B. Weber, 'Fluctuations in Building in Great Britain 1795-1849', *Economic History Review*, Second Series, 9.

H. M. Colvin, *Biographical Dictionary of British Architects*, London, 1978.

J. M. Crook, *The Greek Revival*, London, 1972.

B. Ferrey, *Recollections of A.N.W. Pugin*, London, 1861.

J. Harris, *The Design of the English Country House 1620-1920*, London, 1985.

F. Jenkins, *Architect and Patron*, London, 1961.

B. Kaye, *The Development of the Architectural Profession in Britain*, London, 1960.

J. P. Lewis, *Building Cycles and Britain's Growth*, London, 1965.

J. Lever (ed.), *Catalogue of the Drawings Collection of the RIBA*, Farnborough and Amersham, 1969-89.

J. Lever and M. Richardson, *The Art of the Architect*, London, 1984.

D. Linstrum, *Sir Jeffry Wyatville*, Oxford, 1972.

T. Malton, *A Compleat Treatise on Perspective*, London, 1779.

T. Malton, *A Collection of Designs for Rural Retreats*, London, 1802.

P. Nicholson, *An Architectural Dictionary*, London, 1819.

J. Noble, *The Professional Practice of Architects*, London, 1836.

D. Olsen, *Town Planning in London*, New Haven, 1982.

W. Papworth, *John B. Papworth*, London, 1879.

N. Pevsner, *A History of Building Types*, London, 1976.

M. Port, *Six Hundred New Churches*, London, 1961.

P. du Prey, *John Soane, The Making of an Architect*, Chicago, 1982.

P. du Prey, *Catalogues of the Architectural Drawings in the Victoria and Albert Museum: Sir John Soane*, 1985.

A. Saint, *The Image of the Architect*, New Haven, 1983.

G. G. Scott, *Personal and Professional Recollections*, London, 1879.

D. Stillman, *English Neo-classical Architecture*, London, 1988.

J. Summerson, *Architecture in Britain 1530-1830*, London, 1979.

J. Summerson, *The Life and Work of John Nash, Architect*, Cambridge, 1980.

J. Summerson, *Georgian London*, London, 1988.

D. Watkin, *The Life and Work of C. R. Cockerell*, London, 1974.

L. Wright, *Perspectives on Perspective*, London, 1983.

INDEX